The MYSTERY FANcier

Volume 9, Number 4
July/August 1987

The Mystery Fancier

Volume 9, Number 4
July/August 1987

TABLE OF CONTENTS

MYSTERIOUSLY SPEAKING	Page 1
The Rise and Fall of Gillian Hazeltine By Alvin H. Lybeck	Page 3
Donald Goines: An Appreciation By K. Arne Blom	Page 17
Cornell Woolrich: The Last Years (Part IV) By Francis M. Nevins, Jr.	Page 25
Further Gems from the Literature By William F. Deeck	Page 32
IT'S ABOUT CRIME By Marvin Lachman	Page 35
Mystery Mosts By Jeff Banks	Pages 39, 45
VERDICTS Book Reviews	Page 40
THE DOCUMENTS IN THE CASE Letters	Page 46

The Mystery Fancier
(USPS: 428-590)
is edited and published by-monthly by
Guy M. Townsend
407 Jefferson Street
Madison, IN 47250

SUBSCRIPTION RATES: Second-class mail, U.S. and Canada, $15.00 per year (6 issues); first-class mail, U.S. and Canada, $18.00; overseas surface mail, $15.00; overseas air mail, $21.00. Overseas subscribers please pay in international money order, check drawn on U.S. bank, or currency; no checks drawn on foreign banks, please.

WILDSIDE PRESS

Mysteriously Speaking ...

To immediately end the suspense, TMF *will* be around for at least one more year in the new quarterly format, but not because I have received two hundred commitments to subscribe at the higher rate. In fact—while I hope that other affirmative responses will be arriving over the next few months—I have only heard from 114 of you to date saying that you are willing to pay the higher tariff. (I've also heard from sixteen of you saying that you are not willing, or able, to stay with TMF when the price goes up.) The reason that I am able to announce TMF's continuance even before the magic number of two hundred is reached is that one of the positive responses I received enclosed a check for $1,000 to help keep the old ship afloat. Well, with that kind of vote of confidence, how could I scuttle TMF without at least giving it a chance to survive in the new format. Accordingly, I am committing myself to putting out at least one more year of TMF, and at the end of Volume Ten I will reassess the magazine's viability.

I've given up all hope that TMF will ever attain a circulation of more than a few hundred. Over the years I've tried every promotion technique known to man in hopes of beefing up the subscription list. Once I even sent free copies of one issue of the magazine to a thousand identified mystery fans, trying to entice them to sign up. The response was negligible. At the height of my recruitment activities TMF's subscription list approached five hundred, but it was artificially inflated and dropped to around three hundred in the following year. As a matter of fact, when I set two hundred as the minimum number of subscribers I would be able to continue with in the new format, I thought I was probably sealing TMF's fate—as indeed I probably would have done had it not been for the incredible generosity of our anonymous (to you folks, but not to me) donor.

I can't explain how it is possible at the same time for mysteries to be the most widely read form of literature while mystery fanzines are the least widely read form of literature. I know that TAD has a circulation of several thousand, but it is more or less *sui generis*; the rest of us have to struggle along with subscriptions in the hundreds, if we are lucky, and I think that goes a long way toward explaining the low survival rate among fanzines. It takes just as long to prepare a magazine that is going to be read by a few dozen people as it does to prepare one that is going to be read by thousands; the amount of editorial labor is fixed and is not dependent on how many subscribers a particular magazine has. Production and printing costs are heavily loaded on the front end. As Brownstone Books I produce the chapbooks in house but I farm out the trade paperback and hardcover books to other printers. Brownstone Books simply don't sell very many copies, and I'd rarely order more than five hundred copies printed, were it not for the fact that I can get a thousand copies printed for very little more than it will cost me if I limit my order to five hundred. I am incapable of resisting what appears to be a bargain (even when it isn't one), so I routinely order a thousand copies of books that I know will never sell even half that number--which is why, old friends, a Brownstone Book *never* goes out of print.

What this means is that the break-even point for fanzines is higher than almost any mystery fanzine is likely to reach. It is only because fanzine editors throw in their time for free that they have any chance whatever of keeping their fiscal noses above the ocean of red ink they are constantly in danger of sinking in. Those few editors (like myself) who have tried to keep costs down by doing all the production and printing work themselves, find that the initial capital investment is comparable to starting up a not-so-small business. (If you want to experience true sticker shock, pull out the old yellow pages and call around for prices on an offset press or a graphics camera-- I have lived in *houses* that didn't cost as much!). Then there's the cost of materials. If you want to get a good price on paper, you simply have to buy it in hundred-ream lots. A hundred reams is 100 x 500 sheets of paper--fifty thousand sheets. Chemicals you buy by the cube. Negatives are right at a hundred bucks a box, as are plates. And, of course, you've got to have a place to put all this expensive junk--you sure as hell can't operate out of a closet or even a spare bedroom. In other words, folks, it's probably a false economy to try to cut costs by doing everything yourself; you're better off mortgaging the old homestead and paying someone else to do the scud work for you.

One casualty of going to the new format--more accurately, one casualty of the reduction in the number of subscribers as a result of going to the new, higher priced format--will be TMF's policy of paying for contributions. In fact, TMF's payments in the past have never been more than token, and they have almost always been late (as contributors to volume nine will attest--don't worry, guys; the checks [*heh, heh*] are in the mail), so this will be no great loss to anyone. I will pay for all contributions which appear in the current volume, but after that it's back to the old no-pay policy.

And finally, an appeal for more reviews. I'll need more articles and letters too, to fill the increased number of pages for the following year, but what I especially need right now (and forever hereafter) is bunches of reviews. Heaps of them. Reviews of new books and old books, good books and bad books. Please send them. Now.

The Rise & Fall of Gillian Hazeltine

Alvin H. Lybeck

"It's queer, but the only people who really do approve of my methods are the ones I manage to save from the gallows or the electric chair."--Gillian Hazeltine

Gillian Hazeltine, a fictional lawyer-detective, flourished in the pages of *Argosy* from his first appearance in 1926 until writer George F. Worts dropped the final curtain in 1936. Known also as the Silver Fox, Hazeltine faced a succession of unprincipled district attorneys but invariably proved his clients' innocence in concluding bursts of courtroom bravura. Since his sole book appearance was in 1929, he lingers today only in the memories of grizzled *Argosy* readers. In personal recollections of that by-gone period,[1] Lloyd Arthur Eshbach describes Gillian Hazeltine as "an earlier Perry Mason whom many readers consider better than Erle Stanley Gardner's detective." Certainly it is conceivable, even probable, that Gardner created his own lawyer-detective because of Gillian's reader popularity.

Born in 1892, Worts claimed that most of his life since the age of fifteen had been devoted to writing and to travelling in the Far East and Central America. For several years he had been a wireless operator on Pacific steamships, which later supplied background for Peter the Brazen and Singapore Sammy. Several times an editor, once a dramatic critic, and once a publisher, he preferred the life of a freelance writer to the security of a paycheck; he once said that his only really happy moments occurred when he opened an envelope containing a check, such moments being separated "by periods of the deepest gloom." He wrote a series of Florida stories for *Argosy* in the mid-twenties (under the Loring Brent penname), which were drawn from experience. He functioned in a small town as sheriff, game warden, postmaster, notary public, and commissary proprietor. "The town bore up under it as long as it could, then changed its name." His brother-in-law, H.T. Webster, the famous cartoonist, illustrated a book he wrote on poker. In the

---

[1] Lloyd Arthur Eshbach, *Over My Shoulder* (Philadelphia: Oswald Train, 1983), p. 227.

Alvin H. Lybeck, "The Rise and Fall of Gillian Hazeltine" late thirties and the forties he wrote for the slicks, particularly *Collier's*. For over two decades, Worts turned out millions of words for the better pulps,[1] but he was most generally recognized in the thirties as the creator of Gillian Hazeltine. Close to a million words went into the twenty-four stories in the Hazeltine series, yet readers seemed never to be sated. Hazeltine averaged a story (or serial installment) in one of every seven issues of the weekly *Argosy* for over a decade, peaking at one in every four issues in 1930. As *Argosy* became more action oriented in the late twenties, Hazeltine's popularity grew, and, as we shall see, his personality was altered artfully to tailor a new Gillian, one of greater acceptability to editors and readers alike.

"Lies at Any Price," the novelette which started the series, is a story of unremitting perjury and venality. Lawyers connive and witnesses lie, each for personal or pecuniary gain. Far from a grim slice-of-life, however, it is a gem of comic irony as it depicts the curious workings of justice over a web of falsehood and counter-falsehood. Hazeltine is far from the sharp legal detective so well known to *Argosy* readers in the thirties, and it is possible that Worts did not initially intend him to be a series character. Gillian is described as "cunning" and "hard-drinking," and his history is one of bribing judges and buying juries; he is "unscrupulous" yet "popular with the public" because he is "too smooth to be caught." Nor is this image essentially altered in "The Love Bandit," which resembles a vintage Harold Lloyd movie as Gillian transmogrifies a timid introvert into a seeming Lothario complete with love nest and *inamoratas*. In the third story, a trifle entitled "The Screen of Ice," Gillian unravels a case of environment-*vs.*-heredity to a stand-off because the lies told by the principals counter each other.

These first three stories show a light touch which approaches farce, while courtroom chicanery is given what approaches a musical-comedy treatment. Moreover, the first two stories depict Hazeltine in an unprofessional and disreputable light. This image changes in later stories, but nonetheless certain series constants are established. Foremost is Hazeltine

---

[1] For the record, Worts also had Flash Dan Norton as a character in at least two stories in *Detective Fiction Weekly*—"The House of Creeping Horror" (1933) and "Murder Mansion" (1935). Like Hazeltine, Flash Dan Horton was a lawyer-detective but one who solved his cases on location, whereas Hazeltine usually depended on the courtroom trial. He was younger than Hazeltine and more given to direct physical action—the nickname Flash was a carry-over from college football days and an irritant because of phonetic similarity to Flash Gordon, a comic-strip character. Earlier, in the twenties, Worts had a series character, Dr. Dill, in a series of short stories in *Blue Book*. Dill, an American physician resident in Siam, usually was peripheral to the adventures of other characters.

himself, inclined to stoutness and rather small in stature, with a lean and shrewd face. His black hair is thick and flecked with grey, hence "The Silver Fox," a term which salutes also his legal acumen. He is a successful lawyer, never at a loss for words or ideas, a man who thinks on his feet; in today's parlance, a *winner*. Quick to seek out and take advantage of loopholes or weaknesses, he is a pragmatist with whom results outweigh ethics.

A man's man, Gillian has enjoyed a reasonably active love life. In his later thirties, he has been divorced once[1] and is actively courting two svelte and sophisticated sisters. "The Love Bandit" concludes with him pondering "which of the two would become the next Mrs. Hazeltine?" He has a wide range of friends, many of whom are indebted to him for past favors, and his locale is the city of Greenfield[2] in an unidentified state. Located on the bank of the Sangamo River and close enough to the ocean to feel occasional Atlantic breezes, Greenfield is a city which, though small, is still large enough to have rival bootleg gangs, homicides without number, and endless political corruption. Well aware that more cases are tried in the press than in the courts, Gillian is usually quick with "tips" to reporters and interviews. Addicted to fine cigars, which he thinks aid his thinking, he has an unreasoning fear of dead bodies, a phobia which recurs in the stories.

Throughout the series, Worts does a workmanlike job of making Greenfield real—streets and buildings are localized—and his secondary characters live. In these initial stories, the repeat characters who make their entries include Adelbert Yistle, judicial in appearance, a pompous and slow-witted district attorney who aspires to the gubernatorial mansion; Bullock, his mindless yes-man; Harry Zarrow, the city chemist and a thoroughly venial perjurer (but a man of probity in later stories); Josh Hammersley, star reporter and particular friend of Gillian; Toro, that nonpareil of Japanese housemen; and Marian Lawrence, Hazeltine's efficient secretary (later Eileen Walsh). Succeeding stories will introduce new members of the regular cast, such as Dan Murdock, the incorruptible detective who marries the defendant in "Your Witness, Mr. Hazeltine!" and the incomparable Silky Davis, ex-gangster, who at times is to Gillian what Paul Drake is to Perry Mason.

There is no sharp foreshadowing in these first three stories of the lawyer-detective who is to emerge from the cocoon of shady barrister; indeed, the stories themselves are mysteries only by loose association. However, "The Crime Circus," the fourth Hazeltine story, is pivotal because it is a mystery, not a spoof, and because it identifies Gillian as a solver of mysteries, an enemy of crime, a figure of retribution—*not* a courtroom rogue.

---

[1] We learn in a later story that Gillian has been divorced twice.

[2] The third story locale is Greenboro, not Greenfield—obviously a slip.

Alvin H. Lybeck, "The Rise and Fall of Gillian Hazeltine"

Murder occurs in the first chapter and is not solved until the closing chapter. Of the twenty more Hazeltines to be published, nine will have the words "murder" or "mystery" in their titles and most of the others will have words or terms identified with mysteries.

"The Crime Circus" narrows Gillian's love life to one woman, his wife. This lady is neither of the worldly sisters in "The Love Bandit" but a red-headed Violet (later Vee) Deering, charming, beautiful, and level-headed. A one-man woman, she turns Gillian into a one-woman man. Accused of murder, she is saved by him in a sensational outdoor trial held in a sports arena. No longer a Casanova to be deflected from crime investigations by feminine wiles, Gillian is dedicated to domesticity and to career advancement (when not defending innocent victims from rascally prosecutors). Doubtless Hazeltine's image was revised because *Argosy* had become a man's action magazine—one in which murder mysteries would fit, but not farces.

The transition to lawyer-detective continues in "The Haunted Yacht Club" in 1929, the only Hazeltine to be issued in book form, although with the title changed to *The Greenfield Mystery*. The opening pages, at least in part, might have been written by an editor of today, with their description of contaminated environment:

> Glance at those willows now—gray, dreadful stumps! Twenty years ago all this was meadowland and woodland.... Immediately north of the forty acres of yacht club property were the great tanks of the City Gas Company—monster steel cylinders which rose and fell as though controlled by some monstrous tide ... they were the steel lungs of some steel beast; they sucked in gas from hot furnaces and puffed it out through an elaborate bronchial system under the city. In their mighty labors some of their breath escaped, polluting the air about the clubhouse and murdering the grass and trees.

Also adjacent to the yacht club are the tracks of the Western & Southern freight yards and a tannery. Certainly an ambience for poison is created, and, not surprisingly, a series of arsenic murders follow. Gillian is drawn into the case somewhat unwillingly but explodes the mystery before the judicial bench, smothering the district attorney with ignominy. District attorneys, first Yistle, later the evil and unctuous Mark Storm, were Gillian's natural enemies. Easy to read, the story is fast-moving, reasonably logical, and sets a pattern for future Hazeltine tales.

Following two novelettes, another novel appeared, a gangland murder mystery unblushingly titled "Murder! Murder!" Gangster slayings peaked in the early thirties and Worts never scorned topical slants.[1] Hazeltine backs a budding lawyer, the son of a college chum, and the usual courtroom activity—actually reaching brawl proportions in this instance—follows the denouement. Two more serials appeared in this year, Hazeltine's biggest in frequency of appearance, "Jungle Justice" and "Murder on the High Seas." The first of these takes Gillian to a locale, Southeast Asia, familiar to readers of Worts's other series characters. Vacationing in the Orient, Gillian is abducted by the Sultan of Senang, the world's last absolute monarch, and forced to defend an Occidental on trial for the murder of another Occidental. The most *outre* of the Hazeltine series, this slides into soul transfer and devil worship, but Gillian triumphs at the inevitable trial, exposing the Sultan's covetous brother as the arch-criminal. "Murder on the High Seas," a somewhat longer novel, is a tightly-plotted and gory puzzle concerning a double axe murder on a mysterious black schooner that might have sailed out of a Jack London novel. Here the trial is staged on the schooner's after-deck, and surprises follow as Gillian's cross-examinations startle the court with their revelations.

With each successive story, Hazeltine's shyster taint fades and he grows into the role of defender of the underdog. In "The Diamond Bullet," Gillian defends a young farmer accused of shotgunning a miserly and perverted neighbor. The shooting is witnessed by the defendant's fiancee (hight Nellie Hearthstone!), who morally and psychologically is unable to tell a lie. Apparently outfoxed, the Silver Fox triumphs by, first, having Nellie and her lover secretly married so that she is unable to testify against her husband; and, second, fighting fire with guile, weaving a web of perjured testimony to expose ultimately the killer to be the district attorney (one Elton Drawbridge, not Adelbert Yistle, who is now phased out of the series). In these stories, Gillian's beautiful, red-headed wife, Vee, is a loyal off-stage presence rather than a participant; in stories yet to come, however, she no longer lurks in the wings but comes to stage-center.

In the side yard of a home in a town some forty miles from Greenfield, a vicious old lady and her dog are strangled to death with pieces of grapevine. Hazeltine happens to be present, having been earlier sought out by the niece of the slain woman because she fears the dominance of the sinister and Napoleonic county prosecutor and his cohorts, the sheriff and the county court judge. These men accuse her of the murder and of a subsequent grapevine strangling because they seek control of her inheritance (which will be forfeited if she is convicted of a crime or stays away from the house for more than twenty-four hours). In "The Grapevine Murders," Worts

---

[1] "The Return of George Washington," a 1927 serial, poked fun at the Eighteenth Amendment, having a revivified Father of his Country campaign for repeal. A reporter-detective exposes the hoax, and the story was timely enough to be published as a book in both England and the U.S.

8   Alvin H. Lybeck, "The Rise and Fall of Gillian Hazeltine"

has Gillian unseat the county prosecutor's gang, but only after being beating several times in the best private-eye tradition and after calling in his Greenfield friends to help—Josh Hammersley, the reporter, Harry Zarrow, the chemist, and the redoubtable Silky Davis, bootlegger and gangland figure. In the concluding trial, with Gillian defending Joyce before an unbroken sequence of lying witnesses and a totally hostile judge, the state attorney general intervenes dramatically to allow cross-examination. From this point, the story is standard Hazeltine courtroom pyrotechnics, with a spectacular unmasking of the killer. The lengthiest Hazeltine so far, the story is skillfully written and still is good reading.

"Black Ice," a half-year later, is notable for introducing Mark Storm, the district attorney with whom Gillian will cross forensic blades for the rest of the series. Although Storm's past is that of a legal jackal, he has risen meteorically because of being "right" politically; yet he is not a ward-boss type. On the contrary:

> Mark Storm would not be easily forgotten. His outstanding features were his height, his breadth, and his eyes. His height alone was challenging, for he stood, at the very least, six foot three. His shoulders were those of the trained athlete. Gillian guessed his age at forty. The surprise lay in the fact that he was not a gorilla, not a roughneck, but a gentleman.... His voice was restrained, cultured, suave. Gillian caught a glimpse of clear brown eyes, of a slim black mustache, of white, even teeth flashing in a rather sad smile.... It was hard to believe that this cultured gracious giant was the head of Greenfield's organized racketeering.... He was as poised, as well-mannered, as a British aristocrat. As smooth as velvet. And there was no question about the quality of the steel beneath the velvet.

The urbane and poised Mark Storm was needed for dramatic counter-balance. No longer was the opera bouffe district attorney Adelbert Yistle a fitting enemy for the new Hazeltine. Sterner stuff was called for, and Worts unerringly came up with a fallen Lucifer, a criminal mastermind worthy of the steel of the defender of the underdog. A giant, Gillian must now tilt with giants. In "Black Ice" he learns from his trusted ally, Silky Davis, king of bootleggers, that Mark Storm "has taken racketeering out of the cluck class and started operatin' in it along big business lines"—Silky's own "protection" payments to Storm run to some $8,500 weekly! To distract Gillian during the murder trial, Storm has a henchman pose to the Hazeltines as a friend of a distant cousin of Vee's and to use this pretext to wine and dine the beautiful redhead. Although temporarily torn between the feeling of a jealous husband and the enlightened attitude of a modern man, Gillian exposes the imposter and goes on to win full acquittal for his client.

There is a rather neat touch to "Black Ice" which recurs in later stories. Gillian learns that the jury foreman has been offered a handsome bribe by Storm and will wear a white carnation at the court's final session if he decides to sell out. It is too late for Gillian to start any official counter-move, so he distributes two dozen white carnations to reporters, front-row spectators, the judge's bench, the defendant—and the final one he pins to the district attorney's lapel with a brief discourse on the white carnation as an enduring symbol of purity, courage, and chastity. Naturally, the jury foreman sees all these blossoms as symbols of his self-betrayal and hastily removes his own white carnation, dropping it to the floor of the jury box. From this incident, the white carnation becomes emblematic of the feud between Hazeltine and Storm. They send carnations to each other, Gillian receives a floral welcome at the Greenfield airport made of white carnations, when Storm dines in a restaurant, Hazeltine has the waiter bring him a bowl of ... , and so on.

By now, Worts has fleshed out the regenerate Gillian so that *Argosy* readers are well aware that Gillian is a leading criminal lawyer, a man of national prominence and not without influence at political levels. He heads a large office staff with a tremendous investigative arm, having branches in all key cities; it is through this activity that he obtains essential background data on clients and witnesses. With his wife Vee—"the beautiful redhead"—he lives in an opulent home overlooking the Sangamo River, and it is this peaceful view which sometimes furnishes inspiration for his spectacular courtroom coups. The Hazeltines also own a summer lodge on nearby Lake Largo and generally reflect affluence. Vee is fascinating and vivacious, obviously as deeply in love with her husband as he with her, and she is by now an active participant in the stories; indeed, she becomes a major murder suspect in one novel.

While still at times a courtroom trickster, Gillian now directs such artifices to the ends of justice. In short, he has become a public-spirited citizen and exemplar of marital harmony, one who is accepted on his own terms and abilities by the leading citizens of Greenfield. They may occasionally deplore his courtroom stratagems, but they know that Gillian ultimately is on the side of the angels. In all these touches, Worts has imbued Hazeltine with charisma. The letters in the magazine's "Argonotes" section unfailingly praise the stories and ask for more. (Gillian even reversed time in its flight—although aged thirty-eight at the start of the series, he is thirty-six in "Black Ice" and only thirty-seven in the final story.)

Murder in the country home was widely popular in the Golden Age, and Hazeltine is not the man to be left out. "The Magpie Murders" is an atypical story in the series—no butting heads with Mark Storm, no searching for witnesses, no courtroom or trial at all. Gillian and Vee are invited to Sunrise Towers because of Gillian's widely recognized detective ability. A series of bizarrely gruesome incidents are followed by three murders, crimes for which the inhabitants and guests of Sunrise Towers have invariably untenable alibis. In this story, Vee

10   Alvin H. Lybeck, "The Rise and Fall of Gillian Hazeltine"

ultimately becomes the prime suspect, and Gillian must identify the real murderer to save her. It is a novel in which the pace is furious, the crimes gory, and the characters both stock and improbable, and the murderer can be just about anyone, depending on how the final chapter is written. It may reasonably be suspected that Worts wanted to have some fun satirizing this type of detectival nonsense.[1]

The major point established by "The Magpie Murders" was that Hazeltine is a detective, not just a lawyer. Probably from the viewpoint of a pulp editor, detectives see more action than lawyers. This point is driven home in the next story, a novelette titled "Mystery Over Michigan." Gillian is kidnapped by a leading gang chieftain for the sole purpose of solving a murder which earlier had taken place on the gangster's palatial airplane in flight. Gillian not only solves the crime but also gets the hard evidence needed to indict the gangster. Again, a Hazeltine without a district attorney, without a trial. You can bet that *Argosy* readers were by this point well aware that Gillian was not just a lawyer but also was one hell of a detective.

Another important development in "The Magpie Murders" was the advent of Aaron Savage. The son of a leading judge, Savage is forced by the Depression to leave law school and seek employment, eventually becoming butler at Sunrise Towers. Level-headed, conscientious, and athletic, he is Watson to Hazeltine's Holmes, the confidant and sounding board every detective needs. He figures in later stories, particularly the final one of the series, because Gillian stakes him to completion of his law courses and a job. In time, Savage rises to a high level in the Hazeltine organization, and Gillian later predicts that he will become one of the greatest trial lawyers in the state.

"The Decoy," a high-water mark in the series, is set against the stark Depression background of 1933, complete with bank runs and newsreel cameras. Seeking financial control of Greenfield, Mark Storm has two bankers murdered and exerts pressure to have the banks fail. Gillian, of course, defends the accused killer in a trial with the usual parade of carefully coached prosecution witnesses, each to be discredited in Worts's most sparkling style. During a courthouse lunch break, Gillian single-handedly stops a full-scale bank run by having a newsreel camera focus on the panic-stricken depositors, telling them that

---

[1] Worts definitely satirized—indeed, burlesqued—the Western story at the height of its popularity with at least three serials in *Argosy* in the mid-twenties—"Where Some Men Are Men," "Throw up Your Hands," and "Out where the Worst Begins." These stories are frolics because this was the heyday of virtuous heroines and equally virtuous cowhands; of inexhaustible six-guns; of horses as tireless as they were intelligent; and of villains little changed from their Neanderthal forefathers. Indeed, nearly all of Worts's writing in *Argosy* has a soupcon of tongue-in-cheek, which perhaps endeared him to readers.

the film will show them responsible for the failure of the bank, while simultaneously he has a wheelbarrow of money (actually only one-dollar bills, but who knows?) trundled into the cashier's cage. Later he has the trial transferred to the local movie house and uses the same newsreel film to trap the real murderer. Thus Mark Storm's plans are frustrated, but as usual he emerges smelling like a ... white carnation! Worts's effervescent and compelling style is at its best in this story.[1]

In "Where There's a Will," Hazeltine is the legal Odysseus, quick-witted and able to out-think the opposition. He is summoned to the death-bed of a rich old man who wants his will redrawn, changing the beneficiary from his daughter to Mark Storm (who wants the inheritance to buy a newspaper for political purposes). Two blackmailers, ostensibly house servants, are to sign the revised will as witnesses. Gillian, however, sends one from the room to get him a glass of water while the other signs; this later invalidates the will, since each witness must sign in the presence of the other, something which the testimony of the nurse establishes was not done. Once again, Storm's plans gang agley, and, once again, he is free of any criminal taint. This is an excellent novelette, including scenes in a ghost town near Las Vegas, with a more complex plot than the particular ploy of the witnessing of the will might suggest.

Always fond of current events, Worts based the plot of "The Gold Coffin" on an outrageously illegal scheme to smelt gold coins into billets to sell back to the Treasury at high profit. Mark Storm is of course behind this nefarious activity, but, when the smelter operator is murdered and his corpse disposed of in a billet (hence the title), Gillian successfully defends the accused heroine. The Worts topical touch this time is Gillian's co-defender, a movie star, famous for pushing screen actresses' faces into grapefruit or otherwise treating 'em rough—1934 being a year of high popularity for James Cagney. In "The Honest Forger," a novelette, Mark Storm, ever a master of misdirection, inveigles Gillian into defending a pitiable old derelict who was accused of a minor forgery fifteen years earlier while Storm's confederate steals a painting to be held for a million dollars' ransom. Hazeltine outwits the kidnappers and gets a favorable verdict for the forger, but Storm is unchecked.

A cure for one of mankind's oldest afflictions—baldness—is the inspiration for murder and the resulting complications in

---

[1] Worts was writing at high gear at this period, in terms of quality as well as quantity. Later in 1933 appeared *The Sapphire Death*, a Peter the Brazen novel, and, a little over a year later, *The Monster of the Lagoon*, a Singapore Sammy novel. Both are considered classics of high adventure by aficionados. About a year earlier, *The Phantom President*, one of Worts's more popular novels, ran in *Blue Book*; although actually a suspense melodrama, highly readable, it was rewritten into a comedy for stage and screen starring (if memory serves) Ernest Truex.

"The Mystery of the Five Bald Men." Who killed the inventor's sister?—her brother, his partner, her grandmother, the brutal policeman, a suitor? Gillian finds out in the courtroom with a surprise witness, a 79-year-old deaf man who reads lips. And does the cure really work?[1] "Your Witness, Mr. Hazeltine!" might have been more aptly entitled "The Golden Voice," for the mainspring of the plot is the similarity of voice between the heroine (Hazeltine's defendant) and a telephone operator. Mark Storm is off on a fishing trip in this minor episode. "Murder— In Some Degree" is a medical mystery which again has Hazeltine and Mark Storm outfacing each other in the courtroom. It is faintly reminiscent of earlier stories, with a contested will and murders by poison and stabbing ... and alas, though none knew it then, it was the last of the typical Hazeltine stories.

"Rebel—1935 Model" and "Mr. Hazeltine—Murderer" differ from their predecessors in that Gillian, although in each a key character, plays a secondary role. By the mid-thirties, Worts was discontinuing all his characters, probably because of initial success in his efforts to break into the slicks. "Kingdom of the Lost," obviously intended as the final Peter the Brazen story, started in the 25 August 1934 issue, and the final Singapore Sammy story, "Murderers' Paradise," started in the 16 May 1936 issue.[2] Either Worts was tired of these characters or saw greater financial rewards coming with slick publication. The readers of *Argosy* did not realize that they were being deserted, and for years to come letters in "Argonotes" plaintively asked for Gillian Hazeltine (or Peter the Brazen or Singapore Sammy) but to no avail.

In "Rebel—1935 Model," Worts treats us to a remarkably perceptive preview of the nineteen-sixties rebel. Gillian's niece Rusty runs away from her rich home and comes to live with her famous uncle, whom she "adores." Eighteen years old, she is repelled by the artificiality of life in high places. "They're worried to death about Nazism and Bolshevism.... They don't realize that new forces have come into the world and they don't

---

[1] At least the bald men in the story *did* grow hair. Worts unknowingly anticipated today's enzyme chemistry, since there now is a drug called minoxidil which has grown hair on balding scalps with varying degrees of success (*New York*, 10 December 1984, p. 70.).

[2] Actually, the last Peter the Brazen story was "Over the Dragon Wall" (6 April 1935), but this was an obviously forced sequel, since it changes a tragic ending into a happy one. In the preceding novel, *Kingdom of the Lost*, Peter's sweetheart, Susan, who has been presented throughout the series as adorable but selfish, nobly gives her life that Peter might live—in other words, Susan atones with a selfless action; nonetheless, she is found miraculously alive in the next story, so the series ends on a throbbingly marital note. Singapore Sammy appeared briefly in a minor role in a later Worts book, *Five Who Vanished*, but his swan song in *Argosy* was "Murderer's Paradise."

intend to do anything about them.... The descendants of the pioneers sit around on the verandas of country clubs ... and outdo each other with sneaky affairs and quick divorces, and all they talk about is how civilization is going to pot." Gillian likes her because he sees in her

> a rebelliousness, a wild and unsatisfied longing.... He knew she was hard-boiled and modern. But he also knew if he ever had a daughter, he would want her to be like Rusty—slender and fearless and rebellious against stupid things. He did not learn for a while whether the rebelliousness he sensed in his niece was directed against stupid things or just everything in the fixed order.

It would seem logical to develop Rusty as a series character, either to replace Gillian or to alternate with him, and this may have been Worts's original idea. But after solving one of her uncle's cases by using his kind of trickery, she marries the defendant and settles down to be a farmer's wife. *Sic exeunt* Rusty.

The final story, a book-length novel, is one of the best of the series, even if the defense lawyer in "Mr. Hazeltine—Murderer" is not Gillian but his old mentor, Sleepy Marlow, now an itinerant and carefree drunkard. In the opening chapters, Aaron Savage and Carolyn Walsh[1] are married, with Vee and Gillian as matron of honor and best man, in the summer lodge at Lake Largo, which the Hazeltines deed to them as a wedding gift. Mark Storm, realizing that his plans of self-aggrandizement and of looting Greenfield are continually thwarted by Hazeltine, evolves a master plan to eliminate Gillian by convicting him of murder. The apparent victim is Aaron, slain on his wedding night, and Gillian is framed as the killer, his motive being a clandestine affair with Carolyn.

Half a continent away, Sleepy Marlow, reciting poetry in saloons for drinks, reads of his protege's plight and comes to Greenfield to undertake Gillian's defense. This he does magnificently, aided by the faithful Carolyn, and the trial is a death struggle between Titans—Storm and Sleepy. A key witness, suborned by Storm, is blackmailed by Sleepy into revising his testimony, apparently deciding the trial for Gillian—but Storm's agents subvert jury members to return a verdict of guilty. As with all Hazeltine trials, this one concludes with a melodramatic flourish, the return of the apparent victim. Almost anticlimactically, Gillian acts as special prosecutor in State v. Mark Storm, and his long-time adversary, crushed and haggard, hears the ultimate solemn sentence of death pronounced.

And thus ends the series. The final novel leaves obvious

---

[1] In most of the stories, she is Eileen. The possibility of Carolyn being a sister of Eileen is discounted, since the story states that she (Carolyn) has been Hazeltine's secretary for six years. Same woman, different name—*vide* Mrs. Watson.

openings for it to continue, possibly with Sleepy or Aaron taking over some of Gillian's cases. But such was not to be, and Aaron and Carolyn are left in wedded bliss and Sleepy in alcoholic bliss. Worts had fixed all his characters in aspic, so to speak, despite the pleas of readers. "What has become of such brilliant writers as George F. Worts and W.C. Tuttle?" asked reader A. Lynwood of Sacramento, California, in the 3 April 1937 issue. "No doubt many others would like to see a Gillian Hazeltine story, written in the beautiful and impressive English characteristic of George F. Worts." Over a year later, Richard Frank of Millheim, Pennsylvania, asked, "Where is the Gillian Hazeltine yarn promised a year ago?" (19 November 1938). Earlier that year (25 June 1938) the editors of *Argosy* introduced Attorney Jim Daniels in "Mad Money," a five-part serial. "All you old Argonauts who have been clamoring for the return of Gillian Hazeltine will find at least his peer in Norbert Davis' Jim Daniels"[1] was the claim of an advance notice in the 28 May 1938 issue. But Gillian and Vee, with the people of Greenfield, both the pure and the corrupt, had been consigned forever to a limbo of pied type and crumbling pulp.

Gillian had an *elan* peculiarly his own,[2] and Worts's narrative verve swept readers along. The stories were free of such excesses and lapses as noted in *Gun in Cheek*,[3] and one wonders why more books by Worts were not published, Hazeltine or other. How could Sydney Horler, for instance, have well over a hundred books and George F. Worts less than two dozen?[4] Worts is not to be classed with the great mystery writers, by any means, and it is not to be inferred that a Worts renaissance is recommended. He was a competent craftsman, however, with a high degree of readability, and he does not seem to merit his present obscurity.

---

[1] John Apostolou, "Norbert Davis: Profile of a Pulp Writer," *The Armchair Detective*, volume 15, number 1, pp. 30-35. There was a second Jim Daniels novel in *Argosy*, "Sand in the Snow" (1 April 1939), as well as several non-Daniels novelettes. Even if not Hazeltines, the Jim Daniels novels were good reading.

[2] And considerably more than Perry Mason. Ask any *Argosy* reader over sixty-five.

[3] Bill Pronzini, *Gun in Cheek* (New York: Coward, McCann & Geoghegan, 1982).

[4] Worts was not unique among contemporaries in having relatively few books published. To name two, Theodore Roscoe and Fred MacIsaac were equally prolific and popular, yet each had fewer books than Worts.

BIBLIOGRAPHY: GILLIAN HAZELTINE

Stories

The dates are those of the *Argosy* issues in which the stories appeared. In the case of serials, the starting issue is shown, and the number of parts. This is believed to be a complete listing of the Hazeltine *Argosy* stories, but there may be inadvertent omissions; one may be "Who *Did* Kill Ezra Klagg?" According to *Xenophile*, Hazeltine also appeared in a couple of short stories in *Blue Book*.

"Lies at Any Price," novelette, 11 December 1926.

"The Love Bandit," three-part serial, 18 June 1927.

"The Screen of Ice," three-part serial, 16 June 1928.

"The Crime Circus," four-part serial, 15 September 1929.

"The Haunted Yacht Club," four-part serial, 1929[?].

"A Reptile Named Robard," two-part serial, 1929[?].

"The Lost Punch," two-part serial, 26 January 1930.

"Murder! Murder!" four-part serial, 12 July 1930.

"Jungle Justice," three-part serial, 11 October 1930.

"Murder on the High Seas," four-part serial, 29 November 1930.

"The Diamond Bullet," three-part serial, 10 January 1931.

"The Grapevine Murders," six-part serial, 20 June 1931.

"Black Ice," four part serial, 16 January 1932.

"The Magpie Murders," six-part serial, 4 June 1932.

"Mystery over Michigan," novelette, 5 November 1932.

"The Decoy," six-part serial, 18 February 1933.

"Where There's a Will," novelette, 1 July 1933.

"The Gold Coffin," three-part serial, 24 March 1934.

"The Honest Forger," novelette, 1 August 1934.

16   Alvin H. Lybeck, "The Rise and Fall of Gillian Hazeltine"

"The Mystery of the Five Bald Men," three part serial, 27 October 1934.

"Your Witness, Mr. Hazeltine!" novelette, 8 December 1934.

"Murder--In Some Degree," three-part serial, 4 May 1935.
"Rebel--1935 Model," novelette, 2 November 1935.

"Mr. Hazeltine--Murderer," six-part serial, 21 March 1936.

Books

The Blue Lacquer Box, New York: Kinsey, 1939.

Dangerous Young Man, New York: Kinsey, 1940.

Five Who Vanished, New York: McBride, 1943.

The Greenfield Mystery, Racine, Wisconsin: Whitman, 1929.

The House of Creeping Horror, New York: Alfred H. King, 1934.

Laughing Girl, New York: Kinsey, 1941.

The Monster of the Lagoon, Toronto: Popular, 1947 (wraps).

Overboard, New York: Kinsey, 1943.

Peter the Brazen, Philadelphia: Lippincott, 1919.

The Phantom President, New York: Jonathan Cape, 1932.

Red Darkness, New York: Harper Allen, 1928.

The Silver Fang, Chicago: A.C. McClurg, 1930.

The Black Sander (as by Loring Brent), New York: Chelsea House, 1927.

The Return of George Washington (as by Loring Brent), London: Hodder & Stoughton, 1927 (American title: *No More a Corpse*).

Who Dares? (as by Loring Brent), New York: Chelsea House.

Donald Goines: An Appreciation

K. Arne Blom

Please, don't tell me that comics can't be a blessing. It was thanks to a piece in a catalogue from Bud Plant, Inc., in California that I discovered Donald Goines. It said that the author's famous "Daddy Cool" was available as a comic book, drawn by Alfredo P. Alcala. It was the story of a hit man's fearful vengeance in defense of his teenaged daughter's honor. It proved to be a hardboiled story with forceful social realism. Straightforward, unpainted, unspeculative—a tale from the cruel American ghetto. In all, Goines wrote sixteen books before his life ended in a very dramatic, terrifying, and mysterious way.

The life of Donald Goines ended on 21 October 1974. It had been a good day in his life. He had been polishing his fifteenth novel. By the mail had arrived a check from his publisher, so he was able to support himself, his family, and his narcotic needs for a time to come.

He was living in Detroit, in a flat at Highland Park, together with Shirley Sailor, the woman he had been living with for four years, Shirley's daughter Camile, four years old, and their own child Donna, a girl of two years age.

The end is like a novel that he could have written himself. They were having a good time in that flat. Shirley was roasting popcorn, the girls were watching the TV, Donald was at his typewriter, working over the last pages of his next novel.

There was a knock on the door. In order to find the flat at all, one had to enter a side gate in a hidden alley. Whoever was knocking had to have been there before. Shirley went and opened the door. Outside were two men. They were white. It appears they knew Donald.

Donald was black. In 1974 he was thirty-five years old. During his life he had been a thief, a mugger, a pimp, a bootlegger, a con man, a pool shark, and a drug dealer on a small scale. He had been a truck driver, a factory worker, a shoe shiner, a skittle-ball-boy, and a jail bird three times. It was in prison that he learned how to write a book. During the last five years of his life he wrote sixteen.

His publisher estimates that his books have been selling in the range of a million and a half copies. You find them everywhere in the U.S.--in drugstores, in airports, in supermarkets, in bookstores, even in porn shops.

K. Arne Blom, "Donald Goines: An Appreciation"

It has been said about his writing career that in five years he probably presented the most consistent, the most important, the most realistic literary picture any author ever created of the black way of living, the black conditions of life and the hell of life in the ghetto. Almost singlehandedly he created the rules and the pattern of a new genre that was to be called ghetto realism.

He was born in Detroit and he grew up in Detroit. His mother was a black woman, but could be taken for white. The father was a half-breed—fifty-percent American Indian. And Donald himself had such a light skin that his friends gave him nicknames because of it. He grew up in a rather wealthy home. Nobody had to go hungry from the dinner table. His parents owned a dry-cleaning business. The family lived in an area that harbored the big city's most dangerous ingredients: pool halls, gambling houses, drug dealers, and prostitution. The parents tried their best to keep their son and his friends away from the temptations of the mean streets.

His father had a dream, that the son one day would carry on in his footsteps, but rather than working for his father Donald polished shoes and set bowling pins. He wanted to make his own living. The father had arranged a room in the apartment in which Donald and his friends were supposed to amuse themselves. They gambled and boozed.

At the age of twelve Donald began to steal, and he soon became something of an expert. It became more and more difficult to deal with him. He didn't care for school. At the age of fifteen he faked a certificate and pretended to be seventeen. He was able to join the Air Force and was sent to Korea. It was in Korea that he became a drug addict. By the time he returned home after two years of service he had become a heroin user.

In order to get money to support his drug buying he began to steal more and more. He began to rob people. He was eighteen the first time he went to jail. His life went wilder and wilder.

It has been estimated that during his short life Donald Goines earned more than $100,000 as an author. Most of it he spent on drugs; his heroin habit cost him $100 a day.

And this man spent the last five years of his life writing books, in which he furiously preached against drugs—and at the same time told about social conditions and ways of living that created the need for drugs, created crime and misery.

The first book was published in 1971 and was entitled *Dopefiend: The Story of a Black Junkie*. In fact, however, it was actually the second book he had written. We know a lot more today about the drug inferno than we did at the time the book was published. But it still serves as an alarm bell. It is about a pusher, his victims, and the victims' desperate need to get more and more money to be able to buy more and more narcotics. And it is about the destruction of those victims.

Whoreson: The Story of a Ghetto Pimp was the book he wrote first, but it was published as his second. This one is about the son of a whore who decides to be a pimp and have a fortune, power, and a great car. This book is communicating a deep and shocking picture of the reality of the lives of prostitutes in a big city.

The book was published in 1972, as was his third, *Black Gangster*. *Black Gangster* can be called his first consistent crime novel. It tells about the fight for power in the world of organized crime in the ghetto, about big sharks and small sharks.

White Man's Justice, Black Man's Grief (1973) is a brilliant novel about the American jail system, about the underprivileged black convicts and their powerlessness in their struggle for equality in the face of the law. The main character in this one, who might be called an anti-hero—kind of, anyhow—is called Chester Hines. I wonder if this was mere chance, or was kind of a salute to another great and important black author of crime novels, Chester Himes, creator of the classic police procedural mysteries about Grave Digger Jones and Coffin Ed Johnson.

Goines had entered a period of his life in which he wrote furiously. It is amazing that the quality of his books could be as high as it was all this short time.

It is no wonder that American authors have a very special relation to the dream factory of Hollywood. That's where the big money is. Brian Garfield told me some years ago—laughing with his eyes, before he moved there himself and became influential—"I write my script back home in New York. I call the people at the studio. We agree about a time to meet. I take a flight to Nevada, rent a car, and drive to the border. The movie people come from California. I get the money. They get the script. Then I go home." Donald Goines was also dreaming about Hollywood. In the spring of 1972 the family moved to Los Angeles.

He wanted to live close to his publisher. He also hoped that somebody in Hollywood would become interested in filming his books. Besides, he needed to come away from the ghetto in Detroit. Settling down in Hoover Street in Los Angeles was like starting kind of a new life.

However, Hoover Street is not far from the ghetto of Los Angeles. And there was one thing Donald Goines hadn't left when he left Detroit. That was his hunger for narcotics. He could never get rid of it, he could never free himself from the monkey on his back.

He had become an author in prison. To be accepted by a publisher, to have his books published and to win as an author was a great victory. He got credit for something creative he had done, for something good. He discovered that happiness was not to run whores, or to wear fancy clothes, or to own a grand Cadillac. He had been able to create something meaningful with his book.

But he never got rid of his need for drugs.

Donald Goines wrote his books for his own people. That means he wrote for his black brothers and sisters in the ghetto. He wanted to show the unpainted drug hell and warn them to stay away from a road that was leading to self destruction. His writing became a furious way of preaching against everything named drugs and narcotics.

He wrote with his own life and experiences in life as a base—his life in the ghetto. Taken together, his books give us the most articulate, shocking, and frightening picture of the ghetto ever created. The books by Donald Goines are not like any books by any other black author.

There are many black American authors who have written novels and stories about the black man's conditions of life. I think of, among others, Richard Wright and James Baldwin. But nobody wrote with such anger as Donald Goines. In his books he cried out his pain.

That is why they are shocking. The books are raw—if that is the correct word for it. There are scenes in the books that make the reader's stomach turn. But what one would regard as pornography of violence in many other writers' books is in this author's novels necessary unveiling.

I can't remember any other book that speaks so much against narcotics as his first published, *Dopefiend*. There is probably no other so powerful novel about the jail system as *White Man's Justice, Black Man's Grief*.

It is interesting to notice that Goines was writing during a period of time when the civil rights movement became stronger and stronger. The words of Martin Luther King were still living at the same time that more militant factions continued to operate. Goines might be called a militant author. He refused to compromise. He refused to close his eyes to the cruel truths of life and pretend that things weren't as bad as they were.

He was able to document a side of the American society, by giving speaking examples, a side that many would rather not see. No reader can remain untouched. It is impossible to dismiss Goines as a speculative adventure writer of blood-dripping novels. He points to a social misjustice, unjustness, the hopeless situation for the black people in the ghetto. He forces the reader to commit himself, to become engaged.

In *Black Girl Lost* (1973) he tells about the daughter of a prostitute, about how this girl is able to grow up and with her own hands create a somewhat decent life. She finds in a black boy a life partner, but the boy ends up in jail. While he is serving time she is overtaken by senseless violence. The boy decides that he is going to revenge her. And those two youngsters, who really should be in school, are travelling toward destruction.

Revenge is a theme and motive that is constantly a vital part of Goines' novels. His characters are living under the laws of the ghetto—an eye for an eye. Conditions of life are limited, and there is only one way to repay the evil that people do to people: to pay back with the same cruel methods.

Eldorado Red (1974) is yet another novel of revenge. This book has its roots in a situation from the author's own life. Goines once tried to rob a lottery shark. This is what a gang of boys do in the book. And when the shark himself is starting to take revenge he learns that the brain behind it all was his own son.

Swamp Men (1974) takes place far away from the ghetto, far away from the sparkling, neon-sign world of the asphalt jungle, in the southern swamp land of Mississippi. To read the book is to be hit by a hard fist between the eyes. This is Goines' most articulate novel about the fight between black man and white man, about the white man's oppression, about the black man's helplessness. This novel is a forceful document in which Nature itself plays a spellbinding part.

Never Die Alone (1974) is a technically fascinating novel. A white author witnesses a brutal assault on a black man. He takes the dying victim to the hospital, where the latter bequeaths his belongings to the white man. Among those belongings is a kind of draft for a novel; it is the tale of how the now dead black man made a fortune in drug dealings. After having read it, the author realizes that he can't pity the dead man. He had deserved to die. And the money he inherited from the black man is given away to a home for drug victims. Parallel to this story is running the tale of how drug sharks are destroying each other.

Daddy Cool (1974) is a gripping family drama. In this novel Goines succeeded with the difficult task of creating a professional killer that the reader irresistibly sympathizes with. The killer's life is falling apart when his daughter becomes the property of a pimp. He decides to take revenge. It ends with the father giving his life in order to save his child's honor. This is one of Goines' finest novels; a tragic drama from the reality of the ghetto.

Donald Goines was so productive that his publisher, Holloway House, asked him to publish some of his novels under a pen name. The first one published under the name Al C. Clark was *Crime Partners* (1974), published just after *Never Die Alone*. This is the first novel in a series about a man named Kenyatta--and I will return to it later on in this article about a hardboiled author who must be regarded on the same level as such classics as Dashiell Hammett and Jim Thompson.

Cry Revenge (1974) was also published as a book by Clark. It takes place in New Mexico and is about drug traffic, about gang wars, about racial conflicts, about revenge and the self-destruction that is a reality among drug addicts and pushers. It is as if Goines in this novel will explain that those dealing with narcotics are a special kind of people who have condemned themselves by their trade and deserve no mercy, no pity. It takes so little to let loose violence--and when it explodes nothing can stop it. It has to die by itself after all the damage is done. By then violence destroys itself. But before that, the innocent are also victims.

Donald Goines became an author while serving time in jail. He fulfilled an old dream about writing; he had tried his luck earlier on westerns--without success. It was when reading Iceberg Slim, a penname for the black author Robert Beck, that he saw how a book ought to be written. Goines wrote his books about the black people in the ghetto for black readers. But important literature feels no racial barriers. The books by Goines should be read by everyone, no matter what color of skin. Donald Goines must be one of the twenty most important authors in American literature during the last two decades.

There is a special literature published in the U.S., meant for the colored population. It is not strange at all, when one considers the fact that there exists a black culture in the big country, which in reality is a complex continent.

Holloway House in Los Angeles is one of the publishers specializing in literature by black authors for black readers. They have published many adventure novels and thrillers and hardboiled novels. And they published Donald Goines.

Los Angeles turned out not to be the promised city that Goines had hoped for when he left Detroit. He had been grateful to get away from Detroit, away from the ghetto, away from narcotics, away from the police who regarded him with suspicious eyes whenever anything happened.

He hadn't had a better life in California. No movie was made in Hollywood. He never got rid of his need for heroin. The police became more and more interested in the black man with needle marks on his arms.

Goines decided to move back to Detroit. The road went via Las Vegas. Of course, Donald Goines had to try his luck in the gambling world. It ended with empty pockets. He hurried to the motel where Shirley and the girls were sleeping, woke them up, and had them pack their bags. But the motel owner had no intention of letting them get away from the bill. So the sheriff was called. A phone call to Los Angeles solved the problem, as somebody at Holloway House phoned a contact in Las Vegas who paid for the room and thereafter escorted Goines out of the city to be sure that he really left without getting any new ideas about trying his luck.

He returned home to Detroit, the author of thirteen books, with books waiting to be published and with the knowledge that money was on its way from the publisher when the time came to account for the sale of books. So he went on writing in Detroit.

And he was shot to death on 21 October 1974. I haven't been able to find the reason why he was killed. Or assassinated. Two white men came. They shot Donald and his woman.

Eddie Stone has written a book about Goines' life and writing—*Donald Writes No More*, 1974—but he doesn't give any motive for the killings. The investigating policemen got nowhere, and Stone ends his book by stating that nobody seems to be able to explain the murders: "The ghetto philosophy, 'what goes around comes around,' is the only answer most people can give."

Stone's book gives the necessary background to the books by Goines and the understanding of the motive power behind his writing. It serves as an excellent introduction to the Goines books, and one ought to read it in order to be able to dig under the surface of the novels.

The question is: how come Goines was so dangerous that he had to be killed? Whose toes had he been stepping on? Somewhere there most be an answer and it would be most interesting to get a glimpse of it.

He had finished *Inner City Hoodlum* before he was killed, and it was published in 1975. The opening of it brings to my memory a true story I once heard in Los Angeles. The police had an alarm about an entry and burglary in progress, and drove to the place, a house in Pasadena. The two men in the squad car jumped out of the car, guns in their hands, and saw a young man coming out of the house with his back towards them. They shouted at him, he turned around, and sunlight reflected off of something he held in his hands. The policemen didn't want to risk anything and fired, fearing it might well be a gun. It turned out to be a bread toaster. The burglar was shot to death.

The last book by Goines opens with a gang of black teenagers stealing goods from a train terminal in Los Angeles. The merchandise is to be turned into money by a fence. But a guard shoots and kills one of them, despite the fact that the boy is unarmed.

It is something of a running theme in the books by Goines: the instant and unreflected killing. A person's life isn't worth much.

The killing shot starts a series of actions that leads to murder, revenge, and death, while the reader follows a violent couple of young men—products of the ghetto—and their meeting with a big shark. This is so brutal and gripping a gangster novel that it is impossible not to regard its message as true and serious. Another document about mercilessness—and very eloquent.

Goines wrote four more books, using his penname Al C. Clark. They form a seldom seen organic series of books, each of them ending with a cliffhanger pointing directly to the next book in the series.

The main character is Kenyatta, the most militant of all Goines' characters. This black gang leader has set a goal: to execute all white policemen in Detroit who are enemies to the black people, and also to rid the ghetto of pushers.

The first book in the series, *Crime Partners* (1974), has a scene with a close description of a child assault that forces the reader to stop reading for a while and think, to get strength to read on. The worst of it all is that it is a true picture from the ghetto.

In this book and in the next one, *Death List* (1974), Goines told about Kenyatta and his fight and how he has created an organization that he controls. White policemen are killed, pushers are killed without mercy. The second book has yet another of those hard and close scenes, when it is told about an attack against the most influential pusher's second man's life and family.

The Detroit police force is chasing the killers. Kenyatta manages to kill the big drug shark. But detectives Ryan and Benson are close in his tracks. Ryan is a white man, Benson a black man. Kenyatta gets away, leaves the farm he has been using as a retreat. With a specially selected force he sets out for the airport and hijacks a plane. He is going to force it to

fly to Algeria.
In *Kenyatta's Escape* (1974) we read about how the police force assaults the farm and exterminates the troops left by Kenyatta in a judgment-day-like bloodbath. Parallel to this we follow the hijacking, ending with the plane being forced to set down in the Nevada desert. From there Kenyatta and four of his closest men make it to the Los Angeles ghetto, Watts. After them come Ryan and Benson, one of the most interesting police couples in the mystery genre. *Kenyatta's Escape* functions as a blowout before the final act in *Kenyatta's Last Hit* (1975).

It was published after Goines' death, but written and ready to be published while he was still living and working. Eleven months have gone by since *Kenyatta's Escape*, and Kenyatta has now got himself a new organization in Los Angeles; his goal is to exterminate all the evil forces that are handling drugs and thereby contributing to the black peoples' deaths. Kenyatta forces his way to a final stand in Las Vegas—the same night that Frank Sinatra is having an opening night for his new show at Caesar's Palace. It ends with the death of Kenyatta and the fact that the big drug shark survives the blood bath. It is a book well worth reflecting over.

Who was Kenyatta? A man worth all respect for the reason that he was in charge of a crusade against one of the worst evils in the world? Or a lunatic taking the law into his own hands? But since the law is in the hands of the powers of evil ....

Here we have a black analogy to Brian Garfield's much discussed revenge man Paul Benjamin and the merciless Curtis Halstead from Joe Gores' first novel. We have—why not?—the black analogy to the white world's Dirty Harry.

There are scenes in Donald Goines' book that hit the reader as hard and irresistible as Dalton Trumbo's masterpiece *Johnny Got His Gun*—the most forceful and unforgettable anti-war novel that can ever be written—published in 1939 and years later turned into one of the most gripping war movies ever.

The books by Goines are weapons in a war—they are a declaration of war against drugs. The strange thing is, come to think of it, how all of a sudden in the middle of all the darkness described, there are scenes with warm humanity and softness. This only serves to strengthen the effect of the books.

They are published by Holloway House, 8060 Melrose Avenue, Los Angeles, California 90046. They are sixteen very important contemporary novels.

Cornell Woolrich: The Last Years (Part IV)

Francis M. Nevins, Jr.

The month his occult play "Which Is You? Which Is I?" was published as "Somebody's Clothes—Somebody's Life" in *The Magazine of Fantasy and Science Fiction*—December 1958—Woolrich turned fifty-five years old. He was unable to write any more of the suspense classics which had made him famous and equally unable to produce the sort of mainstream fiction that literary critics would accept as "serious," but if he completely stopped writing he would die, and even though he had lost his mother and was utterly alone, he wasn't ready for death. And so he went back to dabbling in the genres of exotic adventure and horror and the occult that he had explored sporadically from early pulpers like "Dark Melody of Madness"/"Papa Benjamin" (1935) and "I'm Dangerous Tonight" (1937) right up to recent works like *Savage Bride* and "The Moon of Montezuma" and the double-identity teleplay. His next three books after *Hotel Room* fall into this category. But even though they're full of his distinctive motifs and stylistic quirks, much of the legendary Woolrich word power has vanished.

The first of this trio of paperback originals to appear in print was published by Pyramid Books, an undistinguished house whose only previous dealing with Woolrich had involved a reissue of *The Bride Wore Black* in the early fifties under the title *Beware the Lady*. Pyramid paid a $3,000 advance for first publication rights to *Death Is My Dancing Partner* (Pyramid paperback #G374, 1959) and assigned editor D.R. Bensen (1927-) to the project. "What we had, I recall," Bensen told me in a 1987 letter, "was a fairly beat-up typescript ... that we felt needed work to be publishable. It was really pretty awful ... and only the Woolrich name prompted us to do it—along with the fact that in those days ... you could chunk out about anything on the stands and enough would sell to keep everyone solvent."

Woolrich visited Bensen a few times at Pyramid's Madison Avenue offices, but eventually, Bensen said, "we had to talk over some revisions at some length, and I called on him at [the Franconia].... The apartment was old-fashioned, and I guess he kept the shades or blinds drawn, as I remember it being dark, though it was a bright day." Woolrich made strong drinks for both of them and kept the glasses filled during their conversation, in which he described toasting his mother nightly in champagne. "He'd pour out glasses for both of them, then drink hers as well." Eventually, Bensen says, Woolrich raised the subject of money, claiming to be well fixed (which was true enough, considering both his writing income and the blocks of General Motors and AT&T stock he'd inherited from Claire) but "unsure what to do about it. I got the impression that if I got to be a good enough friend of his, I'd benefit handsomely. (I don't mean anything sexually seductive here but rather bait to attract people to alleviate loneliness.) By that time he was pretty well bombed, and I was at least mildly buzzed, but not so much that I didn't feel both sad and weirded out." He didn't visit Woolrich again, "mainly because it was too sad being around him."

You'd never know from looking at the book that Bensen and his colleagues were dubious about *Death Is My Dancing Partner*'s quality. "Tension and terror mark this new novel by America's acknowledged master of suspense," thundered the blurb on the back cover. "Pyramid is proud to present Mr. Woolrich's latest work—a completely original story, which has never before appeared in any form." The book's first draft may well date back to the late thirties, for its storyline seems more in tune with the Big Band era than with the Eisenhower years. Possibly Woolrich had intended it as a serial for a thirties romance pulp like *Sweetheart Stories*, which had run "Deserted!" in four installments during 1938. But the claim that it had never been published anywhere before was true—for once. Everything else in the Pyramid blurb, however, teeters on the brink of consumer fraud. Not only does *Death Is My Dancing Partner* lack all tension and terror, it's the worst novel Woolrich ever wrote. His unmistakable hallmarks are present—episodic structure, feverish romantic dialogue, tinny insult humor, south-of-the-border settings, use of popular song lyrics to evoke mood—but neither these nor the echoes of earlier Woolrich works like "Papa Benjamin" and *Waltz into Darkness* do a thing to save the book. The characters are beyond laughability, the dialogue beyond goopiness, the plot non-existent. No wonder this disaster sank at once in the sea of forgotten stories!

The novel is dedicated "To Chula," the same mystery person in the dedication of *The Bride Wore Black*. We open in the Dutch East Indies, where shipboard band-leader Maxwell Jones (no relation to the Max Jones in the 1947 "One Night in Barcelona") witnesses an exotic temple dance performed by a girl named Mari, who falls in love with Jones at first sight and lets him take her to the States as his main attraction. Jones marries her in order to get her past the immigration laws, but, for reasons Woolrich declines to explain, he has no sexual interest in her at all. He simply wants to use her dance to make himself a music-world superstar, staking his future on the dance itself and even more on the legend that every so often during one of the performances someone drops dead. After one or two such deaths actually take place, Jones and his band become international celebrities. Max still doesn't care for Mari in the least, but just to make sure we won't think he's homosexual, Woolrich has him flaunt a succession of other women in his wife's face—until one night when in her wretched loneliness she takes poison, and Jones saves her life. Now their positions are reversed and *she* starts treating *him* like dirt, just as Louis Durand was treated by the female demon of *Waltz into Darkness.* Finally they confess that they love each other, and their relationship shifts from mutual revulsion to ecstasy. But by this point there have been too many mysterious deaths during her performance of the Dance of Kali, and the only booking they can get is a bottom-rung dive in Panama. Mari decides to prove or disprove the legend once and for all by performing the death dance alone in her hotel room and seeing if she lives through it. This development requires us to forget that the curse is supposed to strike only at random performances, not invariably, but never mind. Mari sends Max away for half an hour, goes through the dance—and doesn't die. Hurrah! The legend is only a legend. Max comes back, opens the door—and drops dead. Curtain. A phrase of the book here and there is touched by the old Woolrich magic, but *Death Is My Dancing Partner* was such an atrocity that even the author's staunchest admirers let it go by in silence.

One of the short stories Fred Dannay had bought after his rapprochement with Woolrich in 1958 was a tale Woolrich called "Newspaper Headline," for which Dannay had paid a generous $400. As usual, he changed the title before running it in EQMM. "Blonde Beauty Slain" (EQMM, March 1959) is a low-key and all but plotless succession of four little episodes showing the effect of a tabloid news story about a showgirl's murder on four sets of New Yorkers from different social strata. It's readable enough (although one of the episodes depends on wild coincidence) but low on vividness and urgency and suspense, the kind of tale that almost any moderately competent writer might have turned out.

In April of 1959 Woolrich made a new deal with Avon Books, the paperback house which in its infancy, back in the mid-forties, had published two of his rarest story collections, *If I Should Die Before I Wake* and *Borrowed Crime.* This time Avon was interested in his tales of occult horror and paid him a wretched $1,000 advance to assemble the collection it released in September as *Beyond the Night* (Avon paperback #T-354, 1959). As usual during the fifties, Woolrich lied to the publisher about the provenance of what he was selling. The collection's copyright page claims that three of its six stories had never been in print before, but in fact two of the three were resurrected pulpers from the thirties.

The book opens with two acknowledged reprints, the complete 1952 version of "The Moon of Montezuma" and the 1958 reincarnation teleplay "Somebody's Clothes—Somebody's Life." Then comes "The Lamp of Memory," which is billed as new but is in fact the same story as 1937's "Guns, Gentlemen," with minimal revisions. Fourth of the six tales is "My Lips Destroy," allegedly brand-new but actually a much expanded rewrite of the 1939 pulper "Vampire's Honeymoon." In the book version, which is set in 1955 and runs about twice as long as the original, Woolrich changes the name of Dick Manning's blood-thirsty bride from Faustine to Nera (hardly an improvement), devotes many more pages to the couple's domestic and sexual arrangements, and adds several touches of true *noir* coloration. The Manning of the fifties is not a stick figure like his 1939 predecessor but a genuine Woolrich protagonist. "I don't know where she came from; I don't know who her mother or her father is, or if she's loved before. I only know I'm marrying her tomorrow. You see her face, and then you know that, and there's nothing else you know or want to know...." When he rejects his simple, safe, and ordinary fiancee and takes up with *l'ange noir*, a woman drenched in uncertainty and dangerous sex and the occult and death, he is acting precisely like Wally Walters, the protagonist of Woolrich's 1926 story "Dance It Off!"--and indeed very much as the James Stewart character did when he rejected Barbara Bel Geddes for Kim Novak in that most Woolrichian of Alfred Hitchcock's films, *Vertigo* (1958). The dark lady of "My Lips Destroy" isn't just a female Dracula as in "Vampire's Honeymoon"; rather, she's death personified, and there is a haunting moment when Manning stalks her through the night, under the tracks of the elevated railroad that still existed in the Manhattan of 1955. "On the avenue she came back into sight again, walking up an endless phantom ladder that seemed to lie flat on the pavement, created by the moonlight filtering through the lattice of the elevated structure. Alternate black and white bands followed one another lazily down her back as she progressed." But all the nightscape poetry can't take the curse off what Boucher in his *Times* review called "the most tedious arrangement of cliches on the vampire theme ever assembled."

The only genuine new tale in *Beyond the Night* is "The Number's Up," a gem of *noir* set in 1929 and dealing with an innocent young man and woman who are kidnapped from their New York hotel room—could this story too have begun life as part of Woolrich's 1958 episodic novel?—and brutally executed thanks to a missing rivet in a numeral of another hotel room's door. The plot device is borrowed from the forgotten 1937 pulper "Wake Up with Death," but this time Woolrich made it integral to his vision of the random senselessness of the world, and the result is one of the few masterpieces of his last twenty years. The collection closes with "Music from the Dark," which is a new title for the 1935 classic, "Dark Melody of Madness," better known as "Papa Benjamin." The overall fault with the book, Boucher said, was that Woolrich for the most part had picked "stories best loved by their creator because no one else appreciates them." But he rightly made exceptions for these last two tales.

As the fifties died and the sixties were born, Woolrich continued to write very little new material for publication and at the same time to make quite decent money from effectively marketing what he had written years before. Books and short stories accounted for about four-fifths of his 1959 income of nearly $14,000 and for about three-fourths of his 1960 income of a little over $10,000, the balance of course coming from sales of rights to movies and TV. Had he not fibbed so shamelessly to publishers, these figures would not have been so healthy. Hans Santesson bought "Soda Fountain" from Woolrich, and printed it in *The Saint Mystery Magazine* for March 1960, in the belief that it was new. In fact it was a rewrite of the 1930 "Soda-Fountain Saga" which had plunged Woolrich into a dispute with Fred Dannay a few years earlier. Since his bibliography was so prolific and tangled that no one in the business had mastered it, not even Dannay or Woolrich himself, he rarely got caught in his lies.

In April Avon Books released its second Woolrich softcover original of the period, touting *The Doom Stone* (Avon paperback #T-408, 1960) as "published here for the first time," which was a flat lie. This episodic novel had first come out twenty-one years before as the *Argosy* serial "The Eye of Doom," and only the last of its four chapters was new. Boucher's *Times* review described the plot with perfect succinctness as, "heaven help us, about the diamond stolen from the eye of a Hindu idol in 1757 and the curse it brings on successive owners in Paris during the Terror, in New Orleans under the carpetbag regime and in Tokyo just before Pearl Harbor."

Comparing the *Argosy* and Avon texts of the first three episodes is instructive, if hardly rewarding. Part One, in which the French conscript Escargot steals the diamond eye from the temple and provokes the dying priest's curse on all possessors of the stone in future generations, is almost identical in both versions, with a few lines retouched for clarity or style. In Part Two, the *Scarlet Pimpernel* episode, Woolrich rewrites more systematically, adding detail to make the story a bit longer and dropping the laughably stilted exchanges of dialogue in favor of a more contemporary sound. ("What is it, think you, a man?" asks A in *Argosy*. "I misdoubt me," replies B. In the Avon version this becomes: "What is it, a man or a monkey?" and "I'm not sure myself.") In addition, Woolrich converts the female lead, Philippine de Sancy, from a sort of French Brigid O'Shaughnessy who uses and cheats the men in her life to a terrified girl genuinely in love with her American sweetheart. Her *Argosy* incarnation had stolen the cursed diamond from another aristocrat in the Saint-Lazare prison, but the Avon version has the old man giving her the stone as a sort of dowry. The Philippine of *Argosy* had first urged her lover Tom Crandall to kill the lecherous Dunot and, when Tom refused, had slit the Jacobin's throat herself while he was lying helpless, but in the Avon text Dunot isn't killed at all. Woolrich reworks the episode's climax in line with these alterations. *Argosy* has the diamond left behind in France but Philippine shot to death by a border guard while crossing the river Meuse, but the Avon version has her bribe the guard with the stone and cross the border with Tom in perfect safety. "We'll find a new little Paris of our own somewhere, just the two of us, you and I," Tom tells her, echoing the "You and I together all alone" song from Woolrich's 1929 novel, *Times Square*. The shift to a happy ending suggests that if one is pure in heart and ditches the diamond quickly enough the curse won't work!

In Part Three, the *Gone with the Wind* chapter, Woolrich adds several scenes and expands others to stretch out the events to twice their *Argosy* length, drops the Southern dialect of all the white characters, and makes it clear as the *Argosy* version did not that the between-episodes owners of the diamonds have also been hit by the curse. In the Avon text the Rhett Butleresque hero is consistently named Ward Waters and the name of the diamond-intoxicated bad guy is changed from Dionyse Bellegarde to Davey Dillon. Our Mr. Black Hat isn't just a damyankee Carpetbagger and a yellowbelly as in *Argosy*, he's also a man of "impure blood" and a "leper"—or rather another vehicle for Woolrich's homosexual self-contempt. In the Avon version it's not a black hag reading the rooster's entrails but a gypsy woman with a tarot deck who prophesies the villain's death by a diamond, and the echoes of *Night Has a Thousand Eyes* and the fortune-telling scene from *Black Alibi* are palpable, especially when the gypsy tells Dillon: "Your fate was waiting for you before you were born." But as the episode climaxes in the duel of honor between Waters and Dillon, Woolrich completely leaves out the *Argosy* scene where Waters had a gunsmith turn the cursed diamond into a bullet, so that the eyes of the Avon text's readers must have bulged in disbelief when the stone wound up gleaming within Dillon's shattered skull without the ghost of an explanation how it got there!

By far the dumbest of the original *Argosy* episodes was the fourth and last. Perhaps in part because he knew this, but more likely because he had to have the story end more recently than 1939 if anyone were to be fooled into thinking the whole farrago was new, Woolrich junked the return-to-India chapter from the pulp version and wrote a fresh Episode Four for the Avon edition. "Tokyo, 1941" tells how the stone is bought from a misfortune-plagued Hong Kong merchant by John Lyons, an American citizen spying for the Soviet Union in the Far East shortly before Pearl Harbor. The moment Lyons returns to his Tokyo home, his long-suffering wife discovers his espionage sideline and leaves him, while at the same time the Japanese secret service comes to suspect him and assigns the beautiful dancer Tomiko to seduce him and locate his secret radio transmitter. Lyons catches Tomiko trying to get in touch with her superiors, forces her to have sex with him, and then kills her just before he's subdued by the Japanese. "For the divine Emperor I die!" she cries out proudly, facing the rising sun. This patriotic gesture so overwhelms Lyons that when his captors offer to swap him for some Japanese spies in Soviet hands if only he'll first renounce his American citizenship, he chooses death instead. He leaves the diamond (which the Japanese let him keep in prison!) at the altar of a Buddhist temple outside the execution shed, and we are supposed to believe that the stone has returned home and the curse is no more. The diamond aspects are so easily detachable from the rest of the chapter that one suspects Woolrich concocted the fourth part of *The Doom Stone* by splicing those scenes into an older story he'd never been able to sell. This last episode doesn't end where it should, with the stone's homecoming, but rather with an inspirational close-up of Lyon's grave, which is inscribed: "Here Lies an American." Shades of Woolrich's childhood reaction to the Stars and Stripes in *Madam Butterfly*! The story will appeal only to those who think *The Sands of Iwo Jima* and *The Green Berets* are the apex of cinematic art, but an occasional passage still sings with the old Woolrich magic. Or, as Boucher put it in his *Times* review: "Few authors would dare make a straight-faced offer of such triple-distilled corn; but devout Woolrichians (like me) may find it surprisingly potable, if hardly intoxicating."

"He called me," Lee Wright said when I interviewed her in 1979. "I hadn't seen him for a long time and he called me one day and asked could I please come up to see him, he was very lonely and very alone, and he badly needed to see someone whom he respected and liked. So I went up. We had tea together." Woolrich likely had something stronger. By this point he was writing next to nothing, but Wright did not encourage him to try harder. "I felt that if he wanted to write books he would. There was no point in my nudging him. And I didn't want to have anything to do with him [professionally].... Because I was scared of him."

(To Be Continued)

Further Gems from the Literature
William F. Deeck

Those of you who may have found a selection or three in this series risible will almost certainly enjoy Bill Pronzini's *Son of Gun in Cheek* (Mysterious Press, 1987, $15.95) and its parent, *Gun in Cheek* (Mysterious Press trade paperback, 1987, $8.95). Both are edifying and delightfully amusing studies of what Pronzini calls "alternative classics," the worst in crime novels. Associated areas--for example, the chapter in SOGIC on jacket blurbs: "Loaded To the Gunwale With Superpowered Quake-Stuff to Make Your Withers Quiver"--are also wonderfully humorous.

Whom do you believe?
   To the frequent accusation that he [Edgar Wallace] employed a squad of "ghosts" to turn out his books he replied merely that it was ridiculous to suppose that anyone who could write so successfully would be content to allow anyone else to do it for him.--From inside back-cover flap of The Seagull Library of Mystery and Suspense (W.W. Norton) edition of *The Green Archer*

   It was ridiculous, he [Wallace] said, to suppose that anyone who could write so successfully would be content to do so under someone else's name.--Vincent Starrett's introduction to the same edition

But he did not stay for an answer:
   It was a little voice and to find its source, Pascoe had to lower his gaze from Chung's Himalayan splendours to the drab foothills where a small girl stood. A fanzine? Pascoe wondered.--*Child's Play*, by Reginald Hill

Even Nero Wolfe sometimes nods:
   "Shall I ask you how you would have seen to eat if your head had been put on backwards?"--*Fer-de-Lance*, by Rex Stout

The menace of the young entrepreneurs:
   There were hazards to walking. He had to steer clear of

William F. Deeck, "Further Gems from the Literature"   33

the three-year-olds on their dangerous peddling vehicles.—*For the Love of Murder [Gilbert's Last Toothache]*, by Margaret Scherf

How's-that-again? department:
   It [the smile] was wan enough, and of course it should be trusting, but not necessarily so trusting that it amounted to her jumping into his lip and cuddling up there.—*The Milkmaid's Millions*, by Hugh Austin

   Spike knelt at the dead man's side and sought for some sign of life....—*The Green Archer*, by Edgar Wallace

   "*Food*!" said John Huby as though it were a four-letter word.—*Child's Play*, by Reginald Hill

   Throughout the trial McCabe made a point of fumbling with various medical terms which occurred in the testimony, and he deliberately mispronounced the words "psychiatry" and "psychiatrist." "Sigh-chiatrist" he called it.—*Dangerous Ground*, by Francis Sill Wickware

   "I have to find out how this blaze started. If it's costive to you, that's tough."—*Where There's Smoke*, by Stewart Sterling

   She ran down the stairs sideways like a crab, her large, pendulous busts shaking....—*Murderer's Holiday*, by Donald Henderson Clarke

   "I wish you would not speak so loud," she cautioned. "There is no guarantee that one of those Yard men may not be a lip reader...."—*Red Dagger*, by James Corbett

   It somewhat resembled the French villas found at Paris Plage, except that the design was entirely English, while in that respect it was unique.—*Vampire of the Skies*, by James Corbett

   She admired that steely glint in his cold blue eyes, for his gaze was fixed on her in mute inquiry, and she wondered whether his glance was hostile or just a passing admiration?— *Red Dagger*, by James Corbett

   He found himself shaking a bunch of knucklebones and wishing that this Sid Page would use a breath remover.—*Death in the Sun*, by Charles Saxby

   ... A cold foggy night in Los Angeles when cars crawled at a walk....—*Death for the Surgeon*, by Gilbert Eldredge

   I gained an impression of scattered masculine paraphernalia—a sporting gun, several pipes, an unemptied wastepaper basket, a few books and scientific pamphlets, and a copy of *The*

William F. Deeck, "Further Gems from the Literature"

Tempest.—Murder Begins at Home, by Delano Ames

"The whole thing is so fantastic as to appear incredulous."—*The Monster of Dagenham Hall*, by James Corbett

Neatest tricks of the week:
The Hound of the Baskervilles ... was but a small concession to the national appetite, for its text clearly stamps it as a posthumous adventure of Holmes.—*Murder in Print*, by Melvyn Barnes

"He writes caper novels like S.S. Van Dine but not as good."—*Death on Demand*, by Carolyn G. Hart

The note had inferred that there might be others snuffed out.—*Murder on the Palisades*, by Will Levinrew

School and university had trained his muscles which laziness had later preserved....—*Affair with a Rich Girl*, by John Newton Chance

His eyes had a defiant whine.—*Poison in Jest*, by John Dickson Carr

Definitely not the neatest trick of the week:
He took bends and corners at a rate that should have spelt suicide, but always he managed to get the car right after hairbreadth skids.—*McLean Investigates*, by George Goodchild

Hisses one doubts ever got hissed, even to oneself:
"I did." Brett's teeth were clenched and the words hissed out. "I did. I know."
"God damn it, Brett." Caroline was hissing too. "You be quiet."—*Pale Kings and Princes*, by Robert B. Parker

"Good God," Lestrade hissed to himself, "they've let him out."—*The Supreme Adventure of Inspector Lestrade*, by M.J. Trow

Then we'll look for the will-o'-the-wisp:
"If the paint we scraped off Miranda's bicycle or the glass we picked up on the road prove [sic] on analysis to have come from a '43 Chevy...."—*Death of a Spinster*, by Frances Duncombe

Well, it's definitely the least known:
41. VIRGINIA PERDUE *Alarum and Excursion*
"... one of the best of the Lord Peter Wimsey titles."—*Westworld*—From Garland Publishing's sales list of Fifty Classics of Crime Fiction 1900-1950

It's About Crime

Marvin Lachman

NOTES ON RECENT READING

There may be many reasons not to like Robert B. Parker. Here is an author who lets his literary pretensions show, yet frequently resolves his books by the "cop-out" device of a gun fight which only shows that his hero is more accurate with firearms than the bad guys. Parker's Spenser has an ego as large as his creator's and an annoying tendency to ignore his client's wishes, presumably because *he* knows better. Forget the negatives. Parker is a superior story teller, one who writes exciting action scenes and has created three of the best continuing characters in recent detective fiction: Spenser, Hawk, and Susan Silverman. Dell has been making all of Parker available, now reprinting a book that has been more difficult to find than most, *The Judas Goat* (1978), $3.95. This is Parker's London novel, and transplanting his not too proper Bostonian to England provides a nice contrast. Still, Parker can't entirely forget Boston, and he includes some inside jokes for those of us who are baseball fans by giving two characters names from the old Red Sox infield: Doerr and Tabor. The engrossing story is told at a brisk pace, and Spenser's wisecracks blend in well.

Nothing about *Looking for Rachel Wallace* (1980), next after *Judas Goat* in the Spenser series, shows a weakening of Parker's talent. Sure, we have to accept Spenser's occasionally uncivil disobedience to his client's instructions and his wise guy approach in always having to have the last word, usually with some wiseass remark. Those minor weaknesses are more than overcome by the splendid narrative movement and perceptive characterization, showing human strengths and weaknesses. There are also some intriguing insights into feminism and the sexual revolution. Parker keeps his plots simple, with few suspects and clues. He does pad his book (and his own stomach) with food and drink, but he's such a fine story teller that I'll forgive him almost anything.

The ubiquitous Mr. Parker shows up again with the introduction to Raymond Chandler's *Unknown Thriller: The Screenplay of Playback* (reprinted by Mysterious Library in trade paperback for $9.95). Apparently mystery collector James Pepper unearthed this screenplay for a movie that was never made; he provides a preface but is not otherwise credited. Parker gets cover credit for his introduction, which is excellent and especially insightful regarding the difference between this script and the later novel of the same name. Chandler cannibalized his own script, written in 1947-48, for his last novel, published in 1958. (Cannibalization was nothing new for Chandler, since his first four novels all swallowed large chunks of previously written pulp stories.)

The Parker introduction should have been an epilogue, since he gives away too much of the plot of *Playback*, the screenplay. It is almost as if he were saying, "This is only of historical interest, so I won't be spoiling any suspense." I suggest you read Parker *after* reading the script, for though this is minor Chandler, there is some crisp dialogue, and the Vancouver setting would have made an unusual background for a movie. The plotting is weak, but the book's main fault is the lack of a strong central character as focus. Philip Marlowe, where were you when your creator needed you? Perhaps it is more appropriate to ask why Chandler deserted Marlowe in 1947, when the latter was a synonym in the U.S. for "private eye." Was this a case of the author, a la Doyle, getting tired of his famous creation? All Chandler completists will want this book.

Penguin consistently keeps Michael Innes in print, even his lesser albeit interesting works, like *A Comedy of Terrors* (1940), $3.95. This is the fifth in the John Appleby series that the author has been writing for more than half a century. Here are many familiar elements: the Christmas houseparty; footprints in the snow; literary allusions, especially to Coleridge; and even a writer playing Watson to Appleby's Holmes. The solution takes some suspension of disbelief, since Innes, following Anthony Berkeley, gives us several explanations before Appleby explains it all, albeit less convincingly than he usually does. Incidentally, throughout Appleby's actions are of questionable legality. Still, Innes below his best is still better than no Innes at all, and *A Comedy of Terrors* is fun to read. In 1947 Innes wrote a far better Appleby book with the similar title, *Night of Errors*. It is based on a plot device to be found in Shakespeare's *Comedy of Errors* and even has a character named Romeo Dromeo. If the various titles have not completely confused you by now, hang in there. Penguin has not reprinted the 1947 book in over twenty years, and I hope they'll make it available soon.

Innes and Appleby are close to their peak in *The Paper Thunderbolt* (1951), reprinted by Penguin for $3.95. This is the ultimate Oxford novel, using the college better than any mystery I can recall. The book is an anomaly: a sheer thriller with non-stop chases, yet peopled with complex people spouting sophisticated dialogue, often in the form of literary allusions. Though Innes's roots were in the "Golden Age," he was decidedly ahead of his time in the use of strong female characters. Previously we had Sheila Grant in *The Secret Vanguard* (1940) and Judith Raven in *Appleby's End* (1945). Now, it is Appleby's own sister who plays an important role. Coincidences abound, but you'll hardly notice them once you are aboard the Innes rollercoaster.

I'm not sure how he is going to do it, but I hope that Joe Gores will figure out a way to make a series character of Runyan, his "hero" in *Come Morning* (1986), reprinted by Mysterious Press at $3.95. He's an interesting, incredibly stoic character, just released after eight years in San Quentin, and it seems that half the population of San Francisco is waiting for him. Only *he* knows the location of two million dollars in diamonds he was carrying just before being arrested. There are surprises aplenty in this extremely fast-moving book. I suppose one could put *Come Morning* down before finishing it--provided World War III had just been declared.

John D. MacDonald's *Slam the Big Door* (1960) is not the first book by that author to be published in hardcover after first appearing as a paperback original. As far as I can determine, however, it is the first non-Travis McGee book to accomplish that feat. Shortly before his death in December 1986, MacDonald wrote an illuminating introduction to Mysterious Press's 1987 edition, published at $16.95. He had previously classified *Slam the Big Door* as a non-mystery. It is the lack of mystery elements and puzzle which weaken the book, but I still recommend it heartily to all who enjoy a good story. It is also a devastating commentary on America's values in the late 1950's and virtually a clinic on real estate dealing in Florida. Also of interest is Mike Rodenska, JDM's hero, who is an early incarnation of McGee. He specializes in salvaging and rehabilitating people and in waging a "war against the phonies."

Carroll & Graf have reprinted two of the earliest (and best) mysteries by Julian Symons. *Bland Beginning* (1949), $3.95, dates from a time when the author wrote detective novels, and it is the third and last book about Inspector Bland, whose name is appropriate to his appearance. Though Symons has claimed he was unduly constrained by the detective story's "rigid" format, this book is proof of how elastic it is in the hands of a truly intelligent author. The contents of this book are of impressive variety, beginning with a poetic tribute to his three-month-old daughter which turns into the briefest of biographies of Symons himself. Literature, cricket, chess, and the academic world are all fair game for the author and are used nicely in telling a good detective story. Reading this book almost forty years after it was published, I found it dated in only one regard. I doubt that Symons (or any other intelligent author) would now call a restaurant "that last resort of the witty and beautiful, where all men speak in epigrams, and all women smile as if they understood them."

I found Symons' *The 31st of February* (1950), $3.50, to be the literary equivalent of a surrealistic painting. Sometimes I felt as if it were a science fiction novel. Especially effective throughout is the author's imaginative use of the calendar. Yet, the true world (London and its advertising industry) is realistically portrayed, and the resolution is perfectly rational. The writing is Symons at his best, e.g., "At a quarter to ten on Monday morning a small regiment of black Homburg hats marched down Bezyl Street. Beneath the hats advertising men were to be found, respectably overcoated, equipped with briefcases, wearing highly polished shoes." Subtle satire and black humor coupled with murder and detection make this remarkable book the best Symons I have read.

DEATH OF A MYSTERY WRITER

VERA CASPARY, in New York City on 13 June 1987 at age eighty-seven. Author of eighteen published novels (as well as many screen and stage plays), she was best known for *Laura* (1943); she also wrote the screenplay for the famous movie with Gene Tierney, Dana Andrews, and Clifton Webb. Caspary's earliest novels were not mysteries. Her first, *The White Girl* (1929), is about a black woman, posing as white, who leaves the South for Chicago. Her fourth (and her favorite) was the partly autobiographical *Thicker than Water* (1932), a study of a Portuguese-Jewish family in Chicago, where Caspary was born. Most of her other novels had some mystery elements, especially *Bedelia* (1945), filmed in Great Britain, and *Murder at the Stork Club* (1946).

SARA HENDERSON HAY, in Pittsburgh on 7 July 1987 at age eighty. She wrote six volumes of poetry which were well received; two of them were prize-winners. *The Delicate Balance* (1951) won the coveted Edna St. Vincent Millay award. In 1960 she received the Pegasus Award for *The Stone and the Shell*. Her only mystery story, "Mrs. Jellison," which appeared in the November 1954 EQMM, was also a prize winner, selected as one of the best first stories in their annual contest. It was a subtly written story about a young woman who sees something in New York City which makes her recall a crime that occurred on vacation when she was twelve.

JOHN HUSTON, in Middletown, Rhode Island, on 28 August 1987 at age eighty-one. Son of actor Walter Huston, he became a famous screen writer, director, and, relatively late in life, an actor. Among his mystery movie scripts were *Murders in the Rue Morgue* (1932) and *High Sierra* (1940). In 1941 he made an outstanding directorial debut with *The Maltese Falcon*, which he adapted from Hammett's novel. Other famous movies with crime elements on which he worked as director or writer (or both) included *The Treasure of the Sierra Madre* (1948), *The Asphalt Jungle* (1950), *Chinatown* (1974), and *Prizzi's Honor* (1985).

HUGH [CALLINGHAM] WHEELER, in Monterey, Massachusetts, on 27 July 1987 at age seventy-five. Shortly after coming to the United States from his native England, where he attended London University, Wheeler began collaborating on mysteries with Richard Wilson Webb; they wrote under three names. As Q. Patrick, they continued a pseudonym under which Webb had written with others as well as alone. Most of these books were about Lieutenant Timothy Trant, N.Y.P.D. As Jonathan Stagge, they created Dr. Hugh Westlake in nine books published between 1936 and 1949. The most famous Wheeler-Webb pseudonym was Patrick Quentin, used for their series regarding Peter and Iris Duluth, the first of which was *A Puzzle for Fools* (1936). The last Duluth novel, *Black Widow* (1952), was praised by Anthony Boucher as "the *'All About Eve'* of mysteries" and was successfully filmed with Van Heflin and Gene Tierney as the Duluths. After 1952, Wheeler wrote the Quentin books alone, but by the 1960s he was devoting almost all of his time to the Broadway stage, publishing only one more mystery. His first Broadway play was *Big Fish, Little Fish* (1961), with Jason Robards and Hume Cronyn. Wheeler won Tony awards by writing the books for three successful musicals, *A Little Night Music* (1973), *Candide* (1974), and *Sweeney Todd, the Demon Barber of Fleet Street* (1979).

MYSTERY MOSTS: POE'S KEY WORD

Poe criticism is about as ubiquitous as Doyle criticism; surely none of us has read it all, even that confined just to his Mysteries, but I believe I have read most of that. So far as I can determine, one of the major foundation stones of our favorite reading material that he laid without credit is found in the title of the very first Mystery story: "Murder" (which he used in its plural form) is what longer Mystery (narrowly defined) stories are almost always about. Although two of his five Mystery stories are not about murders, it should be remembered that his two longest were.

How many other writers used that key word in their novel titles? My search of Hubin's bibliography revealed more than forty who used it more than twice (most more than thrice!), plus a dozen or so others (less prolific) who used it for all or more than half of their Mystery books. This count excludes (except for Creasey) writers of the Sexton Blake books, though most of the more prolific of them used it half a dozen times or more.

Who, then, used it most often? Guy Cobden used it in all seven of his books, the most prolific Mystery writer, I believe, with 100% usage. But many had higher totals. Margaret Neville, Carter Brown, and J.S. Fletcher used it fifteen times each. Miles Burton/John Rhode used it twenty-one times under the two names. W. Murdoch Duncan used it (under his several names) forty-six times, but the champion, not surprisingly, was the prolific John Creasey, who used it (under several names) fifty-two times. (Jeff Banks)

Verdicts

(Book Reviews)

Mary Roberts Rinehart. *The Yellow Room*. Farrar & Rinehart, 1945.

Why is it that *The Yellow Room* is a classic of mystery fiction and yet the name of Mary Roberts Rinehart is associated in my mind with a somewhat Gothic-type of sentimental novel? Perhaps because both are true. Rinehart's books do hold young lovers, usually star-crossed because of misunderstandings and circumstances beyond their control. Yet she could develop a tight plot with much complexity, and characters with real personalities faced with real dilemmas. In *The Yellow Room* the suspense builds throughout the book, so that the reader's interest is held right up to the end. The love element is certainly there, but never mushy, never getting in the way of the development of the story.

The time is the 1940s, wartime. The people are young men in uniform, their wives and sweethearts, their parents, friends, and relations. The place is Maine, a summer colony of large old houses, and its neighboring small town. War has torn this old society apart; some of its people try to keep the old ways going, while others do their best to cope with change. The heroine of the story is Carol Spencer, young and lovely, her fiance missing, presumed dead, her brother a war hero home on leave, her sister married to a wealthy businessman, her mother trying to go on living in pre-war style. Carol, with only (only!) three servants, has come to their summer home to get it ready for the family's occupancy during her brother's leave. This at her mother's insistence; Mrs. Spencer literally cannot believe that there will not be a staff of gardeners and maids to run the house, just as before the war.

When Carol and the maids arrive, the local housekeeper is not on the scene, the house is cold and only partly ready, and there is a peculiar smell, as of something burning. Soon Carol learns that the housekeeper is in the hospital with a broken leg, broken in a fall down the stairs when she tangled with an intruder. Then a maid discovers the source of the odor: a partially burned body in the line closet, the body of a young woman whom no one knows. If the housekeeper knows about her, she won't tell the police, and Carol is prevented from seeing her.

Major Jerry Dane, a soldier recuperating from a war wound, seems to know a great deal about police investigations. He is also much interested in Carol. Yes, you guessed it, the love element has shown up. Dane and his man, Alex, begin a dual task, that of investigating the murder and protecting Carol.

More mysteries—a light in the Yellow Room, where the unknown woman had been sleeping; the discovery of her clothes and purse hidden on the hill; a fire set with kerosene which burns much of the hill behind the house; someone living rough in an abandoned farmhouse. Then Dane tracks the mystery woman to a western city, and some of the pieces begin to fall into place.

Amidst many twists and turns, the plot works its way out. Carol's sister and brother are involved; so are the nearby parents of two other soldiers. The war is responsible for much, from the consequences of dislocated young men meeting none-too-respectable young women, to the tragedies of those who stayed at home and cared greatly. For Carol and Dane, all ends happily, but for others that could not be.

One has the sense, as the book ends, that Carol will never again be at her mother's beck and call, that the world they will enter with the war's end will be a radically different one. Or is that just hindsight? At any rate, sentimental or not, *The Yellow Room* is still a classic, with good reason—it's good reading. (Maryell Cleary)

John Mersereau. *Murder Loves Company*. Lippincott, 1940, 260 pages.

James Yeats Biddle, professor of horticulture, University of California at Berkeley, accompanied by Kay Ritchie, not a girl reporter but a newspaper woman, is on his way to give a rather dull speech, although he doesn't think it will be so, on "The Flora of the Golden Gate International Exposition." They encounter death on the San Francisco Bay Bridge as a careering car narrowly misses them and then crashes into the bridge, causing the bodies of two Japanese men to be thrown from the car. One of the Japanese had already been dead before the accident, but the other dies as a result of the inhalation of cyanide gas rather than the crash.

If this information had not come to light, a naive reader might think it was all Biddle's fault. After all, he made an illegal U-turn on the bridge and his attention to his driving was such that he could see Miss Ritchie's eyes shining up at him, her lips slightly parted. Either she was in his lap facing him or he had his head turned at a rather uncomfortable angle. Whichever, it was certainly failure to pay full time and attention to driving.

The police are convinced that there was only one murder victim and that his murderer died in the crash. Professor Biddle himself is not very curious about the murder, or murders, even though he discovers—and, of course, keeps to himself—a rubber band in the crashed car that probably was attached to the choke to keep the car moving. It is not until he discovers that someone had been messing about with the olive trees he had had transplanted on Treasure Island for the San Francisco Exposition that he becomes involved in the case.

The novel is not well clued and the murder motive seems far-fetched. Biddle, however, is an engaging character and would have been a great deal more engaging if half the novel did not dwell on the joys and sorrows brought about by his having fallen in love at first sight with Kay Ritchie. Among his other quirks are a distaste for mystery novels, even though he had read some because of his great admiration for Woodrow Wilson, whose favorite relaxation was reading mysteries, and an abhorrence of split infinitives, that hobgoblin of small minds. Kay splits infinitives invariably in her writings, but for Biddle these have a peculiar charm. Indeed, at one point this habit saves his life. (William F. Deeck)

Fletcher Flora. *Skuldoggery.* Belmont, 1967, 157 pages.

The Hunter family is gathered together to pay their last disrespects to Grandfather Hunter, who, if he was anything like the rest of his family, need not be mourned.

Grandfather Hunter's daughter and her brood—Hester and Lester, the twins—and his son, Uncle Homer, with his wife, Aunt Madge, and their unlovable son Junior are at the funeral primarily so that they can hear the will read. They are all, to put it mildly, distraught to discover that grandfather has left his money in trust to his dog, Senorita Fogarty, a chihuahua, and to her issue and her issue's issue into perpetuity. The family gets the money only if Senorita Fogarty and her offspring, if any, shuffle of this mortal coil.

Well, of course the only thing to do is to plot the demise of Senorita Fogarty before she finds out what sex is all about. Fortunately for Senorita Fogarty and the reader, the family members are not particularly bright, besides being unpleasant, so their machinations lead to a lot of good, clean fun, except when Mrs. Crumley, one of the dog's guardians, apparently eats poisoned oatmeal intended for the dog and dies.

A pleasant way to while away an hour, or maybe a little less, depending on how fast you read. (William F. Deeck)

Jonathan Latimer. *The Lady in the Morgue.* Doubleday, Doran, 1936; Pocket Books #246, 1944, 242 pages.

William Crane, private eye, is at the morgue in Chicago to try to discover the identity of a young woman who is a resident of that temporary dwelling place and is believed to have committed suicide.

The body is stolen, the morgue attendant is murdered, and the police blame Crane for both crimes. Crane also has the misfortune to be considered the body-snatcher by two gangsters, both of whom want the corpse for different reasons and don't care what happens to Crane as long as they get the body. The gangsters think the body is one individual, while Crane's clients think she's someone else.

Crane and his colleagues, Doc Williams and Tom O'Malley, are on the verge of, if not well into, alcoholism, and the main wonder of the novel is how they keep functioning full of liquor and without sleep. Still, they do manage to find the corpse-- where else but a graveyard--and cart it back to the morgue, where the corpse suffers the indignity of having her head removed and Crane is nearly murdered.

As might be imagined, this is a rather ghoulish novel, but surprisingly amusing also. And not bad detection on Crane's part.

One does wonder, though, how the corpse, several days after her demise and having undergone embalming, for reasons inexplicable--why embalm a corpse that is to be buried illegally?--can still be in a state of rigor mortis. (William F. Deeck)

Francis Duncombe. *Death of a Spinster.* Charles Scribner's Sons, 1958, 185 pages.

Dee Galbraith, trained as an anthropologist but working part time as bookkeeper in a charity consignment shop in Byfield Center in upper Westchester, decides to do an anthropological study of the town. A woman who also worked in the shop but whom Mrs. Galbraith had never met commits suicide there. From the data that Mrs. Galbraith accumulates in her survey, it becomes evident to her, though not to the police nor, I confess, to me, that the woman was actually murdered.

Byfield Center is fairly inbred, close knit at the top, protective of certain of its own, and well supplied with gossips. Mrs. Galbraith's views become widely known, her step-daughter is badly injured by a hit-and-run driver, and an attempt is made on her own life. Someone obviously thinks she knows more than she actually does.

The novel--a first and, unfortunately, a last--is well written, and Mrs. Galbraith is a most believable heroine. She is intelligent but subject to blind spots. She does go to the police, but when they fail to appreciate her information, she continues to investigate. All of her actions, with the exception of her eluding her protectors at the end of the book, are reasonable--that is to say, human and thus occasionally fallible. This is not a novel with a puzzle that most readers will be able to solve, but it is worth reading to discover Dee Galbraith and an interesting study of a small community. (William F. Deeck)

Stuart Palmer. *The Puzzle of the Silver Persian.* Doubleday, 1934; Bantam Books, 1986, 215 pages, $2.95.

Miss Hildegarde Withers is spending the reward money from

the last investigation she was involved in on a trip to Europe. Unfortunately, she is seasick the first few days of the voyage and misses out on the activities that presumably drive a young lady to suicide by leaping off the ship six hundred miles from shore.

Or was the young lady pushed or pulled off the ship? The bar steward is accused of murdering her and takes cyanide in full view of the police. This clears up the case, in the minds of some.

Later on, however, the ship's passengers who dined at the table with the no-longer-presumed suicide start getting black-bordered warnings. Then one of her tablemates dies, seemingly by accident. Another comes near death by poisoned cigarettes, obviously not a fortuitous circumstance.

Miss Withers investigates--and mucks it up, as far as I'm concerned. She also, at least in this novel, is a creature without personality. Stuart Palmer, it would seem, assumes either that his readers will know Miss Withers well and he doesn't have to expend energy establishing her reality or that it really doesn't matter if she's not a distinct individual.

Also not believable is the pharmacopeia aboard the ship. It contains potassium of cyanide and, apparently, sodium of cyanide. What fearsome distempers these are intended to cure is left to the imagination. There is, in addition, a chief inspector of Scotland Yard who tastes the contents of the jar in which the potassium of cyanide is supposed to be. A trifle foolhardy, one would think.

For puzzle lovers--and those who like novels in which cats figure prominently--only. (William F. Deeck)

Glenn M. Barns. *Murder Is a Gamble.* Phoenix Press, 1952; Bestseller Mystery No. 162, no date, 127 pages.

This is a most surprising entry from the legendary Phoenix Press. It is a reasonably literate, reasonably entertaining private-eye novel with a sort of locked-room murder.

Jonathan (Jonny) Marks is assigned by the agency he works for to be a bodyguard to Col. Alexander Smallwood. Part of the deal that the Colonel arranges with the agency is that, should he be murdered, the agency will make sure that the Colonel's killer is apprehended and brought to justice.

The Colonel, it turns out, is a card player of some ability and not a great deal of honesty. He has enemies because of this talent, but these apparently are not the people about whom he is worried.

For reasons known only to himself, the Colonel dismisses Marks, and then is found dead in his hotel room, an apparent suicide. Marks, of course, is convinced that the Colonel was murdered, although no one came up on the elevator to the Colonel's floor, the doors to the stairs are locked automatically each night, and the few other people on the floor appear to be innocent, at least of murder. The police sergeant, surprisingly intelligent in a novel of this type, is sure that it was suicide,

Verdicts (Book Reviews) 45

but says he is willing to change his mind if Marks can come up with some proof.

Marks's investigation is somewhat haphazard, the motive of the murderer is somewhat untenable, and the solution to the "locked room" is a bit disappointing. Still, Marks is a rather interesting character, and the writing is way, way above average for a Phoenix Press book. (William F. Deeck)

MYSTERY MOSTS: REPETITIOUS TITLES

Repetition, as we all know, is as much the soul of the fair-play Mystery as of advertising. In its latter role it is important to Mystery in attracting readers (beginning with the editors, who decide whether books are to be published), and some Mystery writers have used it to advantage in their titles. Lawrence Vail and Julian Symons hit upon possibly the best repetition, with their evocatively titled books, both *Murder! Murder!*

Other writers who doubled up on the use of Poe's key word include Alan MacKinnon, *Murder, Repeat Murder*; Neill Graham, *Murder, Double Murder*; Michael Halliday (and earlier H. Ashbrook), *Murder Makes Murder*; and M.G. Hugi, *Murder Begets Murder*. The allied word "kill" also found multiple double users, including: *Kill One, Kill Two* by W.W. Anderson, *Kill Once, Kill Twice* by Kyle Hunt, and *Kill, Sweet Charity, Kill* by J.J. Potter.

Predictably, most writers who used this technique did so only once, but there were more who did it twice than I expected, and even "triple doublers" such as Ellery Queen (*Double, Double, Blow Hot, Blow Cold*, and *Who Spies, Who Kills*) and the Lockridges (*Catch as Catch Can*, a title also used by Charlotte Armstrong on an Ace Double, *First Come, First Kill* and *Foggy, Foggy Death*) are fairly common.

Frank Gruber (you can look 'em up) did it four times, as did the already mentioned Halliday. Halliday and Hunt (see above) were both Creasey pennames, and Creasey also did a pair with double titles under his own name (*So Young, So Cold, So Fair*, which is most unusual as a triple repetition) and another penname, Jeremy York (*To Kill or to Die*), for a leading total of at least seven usages of double titles. (Jeff Banks)

The Documents in the Case

(Letters)

From Helmut Masser, H. Austgasse 3/25, A-8o54 Graz, Austria:

The recent "Mysteriously Speaking ..." in the May/June issue has come as a shock to me. To be told out of the blue that G.T. is considering not to continue TMF beyond the December issue is hard to bear; his wish to stop TMF's publication betrays a savage and brutal determination (probably acquired at law school).
Why can't idealists stay idealists forever?
Having created a flourishing magazine, a devoted following of TMF lovers, a community of friends (as Frank Floyd has recently put it in a letter) G.T. still seems to feel entitled to some leisure time, to making money, to putting an end to subsidizing overseas subscribers. He seems to think he can withdraw our criminous drug just like that, leaving us out in the cold without our beloved magazine.
I, for my part, won't put up with it; I'd rather come up with $35.00 to keep the boat afloat.
But what if friends aren't friends after all?
What if their addiction is not strong enough and they fail to raise the money? Then let this letter be a lament for past joys ....
I well remember the day when I received the preview issue in the mail (and I have kept hoping since then that one day it, too, will become a collector's item putting me among the rich). I remember how excited I was in those pioneering days when TMF was a giant-size mag, hard to read because of the funny ink G.T. was experimenting with, and issued on paper of a different colour every time.
Let me fondle my TMFs 6/6 and 7/1 with their great (pulpy) covers, or 7/6 when TMF went spicy (on the cover at least).
May I remind you of 8/3, with a letter of temporary suspension accompanying it (a "rare, hard to locate item" as the collectors have it).
How thrilling having had to consult a map every other issue in order to trail G.T. across the continent.
And then in more recent days G.T.'s battle against a fellow

The Documents in the Case (Letters)

publisher for a more liberal view towards those who refused to fight in Vietnam. We all left the realm of the cozy library or mean streets for a while, knowing that bigger issues were at stake.

I remember a bloke saying "When a guy's number's come up, it's come up, it's just that," without questioning a person's or a government's right to make *your* number come up.

It was TMF that put the question.

We can't afford to let the magazine die; for its loss we wouldn't feel sweet nostalgia but bitter regret.

From William F. Deeck, 9020 Autoville Drive, College Park, MD 20740:

Victor McLaglen, in *She Wore a Yellow Ribbon*, was asked as something of an authority on whisky, to taste a highly inflammable liquid purported to be whisky and render an opinion. He opined: "It's better than no whisky at all." Which is my opinion of TMF's going quarterly rather than folding. Some TMF is better than no TMF. There are far too few fanzines in existence. We can't afford to lose one. I hope 199 other people agree with me.

Maryell Cleary's study of contemporary detectives also involved in religious life is excellent. Perhaps now she'll think about surveying those who unfortunately are long out of print. I've recently started reading Margaret Scherf's novels featuring Martin Buell and have found them most enjoyable. The non-Buell novels of hers, on the other hand, I have to judge mediocre.

Frank Floyd asks which were the best Perry Mason novels. Thirty years ago I read all of them as they were published in paperback, and after reading about twenty I discovered I was beginning to be unable to tell them apart. Thus, I couldn't cast a vote.

Fanciers of Margery Allingham should be delighted with Barry Pike's *Campion's Career: A Study of the Novels of Margery Allingham* (Bowling Green University Popular Press, 1987). If there is a weakness in Pike's study, it is that it made me want to stop reading about the novels and reread the novels instead. But that also is its strength. Highly recommended for those who like to read *about* the literature as well as read the literature itself. Which, I guess, is all of TMF's readership.

From Maryell Cleary, Box 155, Lyons, OH 43533:

I do hope that you get enough expressions of willingness to subscribe at the new rate for you to continue TMF. There are few of the general, all 'round, all-purpose mystery fan magazines these days. *The Poisoned Pen* comes out so rarely and irregularly that it's impossible to count on it. *MRA Journal* is good, but has a specific focus for each issue. *Mystery Scene* and *MDM* are specialized publications. That leaves TMF and

TAD. If TMF drops out, I'll be driven back to TAD, which I object to because it accepts articles and holds them for years without printing them. TMF has those neat features by Marv Lachman, Bill Deeck, Walter Albert, and Jeff Banks. How can I live without them? I'd like to see more reviews and letters, but that's something that can happen.

I'd like to know something about the inner working of publishing a fan magazine. How do you get articles? Are you swamped by them or do you have to armtwist to get them? Are there many people who subscribe but never write a letter, review, or article? Do libraries ever take subscriptions? How do fans learn about fan magazines?

No, I'm not thinking of starting one myself. I'm not that kind of masochist. I've edited a small professional publication and know about the hassles with mailing lists, money, getting material on time, etc. Editing can be fun, but all the rest, as far as I'm concerned, is a big pain.

It is a mystery to me why so many people read mysteries and love them, but aren't the least bit interested in collateral activities. Some of my best friends .... I wonder how other people get involved in fandom? For me it all started with an ad for a used booklist in EQMM. Would other readers be willing to share how they got involved?

From R. Jeff Banks, P.O. Box 13007, SFA Station, Nacogdoches, TX 75962:

Since I am writing you anyway, I am returning the postcard unused—save a few pennies by recycling it whenever you need another. My one-word answer is, of course, YES.

However, as I have the space, I'm going to qualify that just a bit. I stopped taking TAD when the price went to more than I could afford, and that price was lower than your projected one. However, I will not stop taking TMF. Why not, for instance, stop paying contributors? I have argued over and over that we who write for you would do it just as consistently (and carefully) without pay; I really believe that. Certainly in my teaching situation, research time that I have spent on Mystery articles could have been spent on more traditional English-teachery type research and had some small chance of favorably impacting my small wage. And I will add to that that my typical amount of time spent on an MM page could have produced a 4-6 page article on Mystery or some obscure passage of Chaucer or Shakespeare. The reason I have chosen to devote the time to Mystery research (and frequently specifically to the MM project) is my greater love for the subject(s). At your word rates, nobody can be doing the writing for the pay.

Of course, you will rightly respond that your expense for material is only a tiny drop in the total expense bucket (and will become the tinier as your other expenses rise). True, I am sure, but still I am sure other spots to economize could be found.

On to happier (than money) topics:

The Documents in the Case (Letters)

I certainly enjoyed this latest issue, not the least reason being that my filler pieces seem to be "filling the bill" as designed. I am grateful for the addenda and corrections offered by several readers, and I am updating/correcting my little essays in my files.

The clergy-detectives article was certainly the more effective for being "complete in one issue." But I do hope that if you do go to the larger word count format you will not opt always for longer articles. The short ones (and I'm not here referring to my fillers) are a sort of trademark for TMF, and I generally prefer them.

From Richard West, 1918 Madison Street, Madison, WI 53711:

I can understand your wanting to wrap up TMF and go on to other things. But if you decide to continue, I'll certainly stay with you.

Footnote to Maryell Cleary's article on "Contemporary Clergy-Detectives": Leonard Holton was a pseudonym for Leonard Wibberley, now unhappily deceased. So there is indeed no likelihood of a continuation of the Fr. Brodder series.

From Walker Martin, 432 Latona Ave., Trenton, NJ 08618:

The thought of TMF ceasing publication *again* makes my blood run cold! I managed to survive the first time and felt we were all safe. Don't you realize TMF is a pure labor of love? Sacrifice your job, family, your reputation, but not TMF. Long after we are all dead and gone your magazine will still be lurking in used book stores and mystery collections. It's probably the most important thing you are doing! But in answer to your question, yes, I will pay extra for the new size.

From Charles Shibuk, 2084 Bronx Park East, Bronx, NY 10462:

Alas, Jeff Banks errs again. Christopher Bush's series detective is Ludovic Travers (not Peters). Ludovic Peters is a British mystery writer.

I must admit to being at a complete loss to understand how anyone could ever call this detective a "British Philo Vance."

Furthermore, I simply cannot believe that Marv Lachman in his review of *The Bride Wore Black* called this tale "Woolrich's first novel." It was his seventh--but first *mystery* novel.

I personally suspect editorial error of a high order.

Happy 20th Birthday, TAD!

Celebrate TAD's first two decades with this money-saving combination: a hardcover facsimile reprint of TAD's first volume and a trade paperback collection of eighteen essays and reminiscences on TAD's early days by founder Al Hubin and more than a dozen other luminaries who made it all happen. Both books—a $29.95 value—are available direct from Brownstone Books for $25.00 postpaid. Save $4.95 and treat yourself to hours of pleasurable reading in the company of TAD's leading lights:

> *The Armchair Detective*, Volume One, smythe-sewn and bound in quality cloth, this facsimile reprint contains all 158 pages of the first four issues of TAD, plus a specially written Introduction by Allen J. Hubin; viii, 158 pp., available individually for $17.00 postpaid.

> *TAD-SCHRIFT: Twenty Years of Mystery Fandom in The Armchair Detective*, edited by J. Randolph Cox, this quality trade paperback contains essays by Bob Adey, Jon L. Breen, Robert E. Briney, Joe R. Christopher, J. Randolph Cox, William K. Everson, John A. Hogan, Estelle Fox, Marvin Lachman, Edward S. Lauterbach, Frank D. McSherry, Jr., Francis M. Nevins, Jr., William F. Nolan, John Bennett Shaw, Charles Shibuk, Donald A. Yates, and a long survey of TAD's first decade by founder and long-time editor Allen J. Hubin; vii, 111 pp., available individually for $12.95 postpaid.

Also Available from Brownstone Books

Detective and Mystery Fiction: An International Bibliography of Secondary Sources, edited by Walter Albert, smythe-sewn and bound in quality cloth, this Edgar winner belongs on the reference shelf of every mystery fan worthy of the name; xii, 781 pp., $60.00 postpaid.

The Sound of Detection: Ellery Queen's Adventures in Radio, edited by Francis M. Nevins, Jr., and Ray Stanich, this illustrated, quality trade paperback, which consists of a detailed narrative history (by Nevins) of the long-running Ellery Queen radio program and an annotated log (by Stanich and Nevins) of the individual episodes, is a must for Queen fans as well as fans of Old Time Radio; viii, 109 pp., $6.95 postpaid.

The Mystery Fancier, second oldest generalist mystery fan publication in the United States (only TAD has been around longer), is now published quarterly in a trade-paperback format. A year's subscription is $25.00 (second class), $30.00 (first class in U.S. and Canada), or $35.00 (airmail overseas). Individual issues are $7.50 postpaid.

In the Brownstone Chapbook Series

Volume One: *Hardboiled Burlesque: Raymond Chandler's Comic Style*, by Keith Newlin, 50 pp., $4.95 postpaid.

Volume Two: *The New Hard-Boiled Dicks: A Personal Checklist*, by Robert E. Skinner, vii, 60 pp., $6.95 postpaid.

Volume Three: *John Nieminski: Somewhere a Roscoe*, selected and edited by Ely Liebow and Art Scott, 61 pp., $6.95 postpaid.

Brownstone Books
407 Jefferson Street
Madison, Indiana 47250
(812/265-2636)

www.ingramcontent.com/pod-product-compliance
Lightning Source LLC
Chambersburg PA
CBHW031434040426
42444CB00006B/805